Other Books by

Melissa also writes children's books under the pen name Emmy Donovan.

Adventures in Writing

Ready, Set, Write:
A Guide to Creative Writing

Melissa Donovan

Swan Hatch Press | San Francisco

Adventures in Writing
Ready, Set, Write: A Guide to Creative Writing

First Edition, 2019
Published by Swan Hatch Press • Melissa Donovan

ISBN 10: 0-9976713-3-5
ISBN 13: 978-0-9976713-3-9

Library of Congress Control Number: 2019903089

Adventures in Writing

Ready, Set, Write:
A Guide to Creative Writing

Contents

Introduction:
Getting Ready to Write

When I was a little girl, my mom used to sit, curled up on the couch, with a thick paperback novel in her hands and a big bag of M&Ms in her lap. I'm still trying to quit my candy habit! But books are forever.

My mom taught me to read by the time I turned four. The rhyming stories of Dr. Seuss were among my early favorites. Soon I was devouring *Charlotte's Web* and *Little House in the Big Woods*. Later it was the Narnia books and *A Wrinkle in Time*. I constantly checked out *Where the Sidewalk Ends* from my school library. Whenever I asked for new books, my mom would take me to the used paperback store and let me pick out a few. Whenever the Scholastic newsletter came, she let me order a few books from the catalog. And whenever I asked to go to the big public library, she drove me there.

When I was about thirteen years old, something changed. After years of reading other people's words, I started putting my own words on the page.

They were poems or songs, inspired by the music that I loved and informed by the books I had read. I composed these pieces in my spiral-bound notebook, which was intended for schoolwork. I remember marveling at the words I'd written. I had created something—and I had done it with nothing more than a pen and paper and some words. I was elated. I wanted to write more.

Around the same time, one of my teachers required our class to keep journals. We wrote in our journals for a few minutes every day, and when the semester ended, I continued writing in mine throughout the summer and for years afterward.

I filled many notebooks throughout my teens and early twenties. I wrote about my thoughts and feelings. I explored ideas. I wrote poems and personal essays. I composed song lyrics. Later, I started to tinker with storytelling.

I sometimes hear people talk about what it means to be a "real writer." Occasionally, someone will say that a "real writer" loves to write, needs to write, or gets paid to write.

I disagree.

I'm a real writer because I write. Sure, sometimes I love it, but not always. Other times, I need to do it, but not always. Sometimes I get paid to write, but that didn't happen until many years after I'd started writing. There are times when writing is frustrating, exhausting, or just plain difficult. I've experienced writer's block. I've struggled with doubt and dismay about my work. I've taken long, unplanned breaks from writing.

But I always come back.

Writing is part of who I am. It's what I do.

If you're reading this, you're probably a writer, too. At the very least, you're an aspiring writer. That doesn't mean you intend to get your name on a best-seller list (although you might). It doesn't mean you plan to get paid for your writing (although you might). It doesn't mean you will submit your work and get it published (although you might).

It just means you want to write.

And so you should.

What You'll Find Inside This Book

As the title implies, this book is a guide to creative writing.

It isn't a book that delves into grammar, spelling, or punctuation. It doesn't tell you how to become a professional, published author. It does one thing and one thing only: shows you what you can write and how you can write it.

You'll start by creating a space in which to write. Then you'll explore various forms of writing that you can experiment with in your new writing space. You'll answer some questions about writing. You'll try some writing activities. You'll learn techniques to help you stay motivated and inspired. Finally, you'll put together your own writer's tool kit.

You might want to try some forms of writing but skip others. When you find questions at the end of a chapter, you might want to answer one, or none, or all of them. You might want to skip ahead and read about a topic that interests you. Do what feels comfortable; you can (and should) use this book in any way you like.

But if you're looking for suggestions, I'd recommend reading one chapter a day. The chapters are intentionally short, and you'll find questions and activities to prompt a writing session at the end of each chapter. So get your notebook ready.

Get Ready to Write

I hope you'll keep an open mind as you make your way through this book. Try different forms and genres. Use a variety of tools and techniques. Take risks, and don't expect everything to come easily, but know that your efforts will be rewarded.

The more you explore and experiment, the more fun you'll have and the better your writing will become. I hope this book will encourage, inspire, and inform you on your writing adventure.

Activity: Get Set

If you talk to enough writers, you'll soon find that we each have our own habits and rituals, our own talents and challenges. Some people rise early and dedicate an hour each day to the craft, while others only put pen to paper when inspiration strikes. Some people like to write in a café, with a notebook and a pen. Others dedicate an entire room to their writing, furnishing it with bookshelves and a desk with a laptop, a stack of notepads, and a cup of pens. Some writers keep everything neat and organized. Others are messy. There are writers who suffer from imposter syndrome, feeling like they have no right to put their words on the page, while others easily let their ideas flow to a blinking cursor on a computer screen.

As you make your way through your writing journey, you'll discover your strengths and weaknesses. You'll unearth talents that you didn't know you possessed and challenges that you never imagined facing. You'll acquire tools that work for you and develop practices that produce satisfying results so your writing reaches its full potential.

For now, though, all that matters is that you do the one thing all writers do: write. Which means you need a place to put your words.

Activity: Create a Writing Space

For your first activity, create a writing space for yourself—a place where you'll put your words.

I recommend starting with the tried-and-true method of writing longhand in a notebook with a pen. There's something about the tactile experience of writing in a notebook that seems to boost creativity.

We writers tend to have an affinity for lovely journals with slick hardback covers and thick, archival-quality pages. But such tools can quickly become precious, and that makes them restrictive. Who wants to jot down random notes and bizarre ideas into such an exquisite object? It should be saved for a masterpiece!

But writing is gritty. It's messy and often disorganized. As you discover your writing, you need to allow yourself to make mistakes, to write poorly, and to produce pages that will never be looked upon by any eyes other than your own. You need to write in a notebook that you would drag through the mud without fretting. A composition notebook or a spiral-bound is just the thing!

But that's just my recommendation; it's certainly not a requirement. If you prefer a fancy journal, by all means, use one.

Of course, you can also use a computer. There are several advantages to this approach. You can write faster (if you know how to type), and it's easier to edit your work and organize your files on a computer. Just create a directory where you can stash your writing, make sure you have a word-processing program installed, and you'll be ready to go.

Personally, I use a combination of notebooks and a computer, depending on what I'm writing. But that's just me. The important thing is that you stake your claim to a writing space and give yourself permission to write.

You'll use this new writing space for the questions, exercises, and activities that you'll find throughout this book.

You might want to go beyond this book and write other things—by all means, do so. It's your writing space. Use it.

Part I: What is Creative Writing?

1

What is Creative Writing?

Creative writing can be difficult to define.

Certainly, fiction and poetry are forms of creative writing, but what about journal writing, articles and essays, memoirs and biographies? What about textbooks and copywriting? Technical writing? Blog posts?

Where do we draw the line between creative writing and other types of writing?

In some cases, what qualifies as creative is obvious. You read something, and you know a lot of creativity went into it. Other times, a piece of writing, while skillful, might not strike you as creative in nature. And then there's everything in between—stuff that's sort of creative or not quite creative enough.

Fiction is made-up stuff borne of the imagination. Poetry takes artistic liberties with language and imagery. These types of writing require a significant level of creative thinking. But many other types of writing are creative as well. When you read a memoir with beautiful turns of phrase or an essay that evokes an emotional response, you're experiencing the writer's creativity. Conversely, dry, factual material, such as a user's guide, might be completely lacking in artistry.

Have you ever read the terms and conditions on a website? Ever browsed through an instruction manual? Surely, you've suffered through a boring textbook. While these types of writing might require some level of creativity, they are not usually considered creative writing.

It's easy to glance at a poem and know that it's a piece of creative writing, and it's easy to flip through a legal document and know that it's not.

So what is creative writing?

If a textbook is not creative writing, then wouldn't that exclude other nonfiction works, such as memoirs and biographies, from creative writing?

Not necessarily.

While nonfiction indicates that the writing is rooted in fact, it can be written with emphasis on language and craftsmanship and therefore creative. Creative nonfiction is a broad genre that includes memoirs and biographies, personal essays, travel and food writing, and literary journalism.

Ultimately, we each get to decide what is art and what is creative writing. Most of us will know creative writing when we experience it, either as a writer or as a reader.

In the big scheme of things, it may not be that important to go around labeling what is and isn't creative writing, but it's certainly worthy of a few brief moments of consideration. You can determine what creative writing is for yourself, but others might see things differently.

Questions

Do you differentiate between creative writing and other types of writing? Do you feel that copywriting (ads, commercials, etc.) can be classified as creative writing even though its purpose is strictly commercial? If most textbooks are not considered creative writing, does that mean a textbook can never be written creatively? Is writing creative because of how the writer approaches the project, or how the reader receives it?

2

Why We Write

There are many reasons to write. Maybe you feel a need to express yourself. Perhaps you use writing to clear your mind or figure out what you think or how you feel about something. You might write because you're gripped by ideas and images, and writing allows you to explore them. Maybe you use writing as a tool for some other objective: sharing your ideas, experiences, or knowledge with others. Or perhaps you want to make a career of it, to use writing as a way to support yourself.

There's no right or wrong reason to write—and there's no good or bad reason to write. If you are compelled to put words on the page, then you should put words on the page.

At its core, writing is a form of communication, a way to connect with an audience. Some people have been fundamentally changed by a speech, a novel, or a poem. Almost everyone has been moved by a story or a song. And a few have been persuaded to new viewpoints or motivated to engage in some action or activity by the sheer act of reading what another person has written. In the hands of a passionate and skilled writer and in front of a willing and ready audience, a piece of writing can shake the world

But not all words are written to be shared. Many people use writing for self-expression or even for therapeutic purposes.

Troubling emotions are often alleviated by putting them into words: feelings of rage, sorrow, pain, and suffering. And this gives writing an even greater power: the power to heal, to bring about inner peace and wellness.

Therapeutic writing doesn't have to focus on the negative. For example, a daily gratitude journal emphasizes the good things in life, promoting a healthy attitude and positive outlook on the world.

And sometimes writing is just plain fun. You can make language dance. You can create worlds. You can explore the past and invent the future.

All for the cost of a pen and a notebook.

What is a Writer?

Occasionally you'll hear people arguing that you can't be a writer until you've earned money from writing, or that a real writer is someone who would die of heartache if they stopped writing. This is hyperbole, pure nonsense.

A writer is someone who writes, someone who uses the written word to communicate with others or express their ideas. A writer writes regularly but might not write frequently. Some writers write a lot. Some write a little. But all writers do one thing: we write.

Nobody gets to tell you how to be a writer. Nobody gets to invalidate your reasons for writing, or what you're writing, or how you're writing. Nobody gets to tell you when or where to write.

Who Do You Write For?

I tend to think of an author as someone who has written professionally, for an audience.

Many people write for nobody other than themselves. They keep journals or diaries that are never seen by another pair of eyes, or they write and publish books, caring little if anyone reads or even likes their work.

But many writers yearn for readers or want to make a career of writing, even if it's only some extra income on the side. They write for an audience. The audience might change over time. First, we write for ourselves, then perhaps for our friends and family. Later, we might put our writing in front of a small audience—on a blog or in a workshop. Eventually, we reach out to agents and editors. Finally, we seek a readership, people who will pay to read what we have written.

Whether you only write for yourself or you've set a goal to become a professional, published author, it's up to you to decide why you write and who you're writing for.

Questions

Are you a writer? Do you want to become a professional author? Why do you write? Who do you write for?

3

How We Write

As a writer, it's helpful to figure out two things about yourself: your working style and your goals. Understanding your working style and knowing your goals will be essential in guiding you through the jungle of writing advice that you'll find in various writing resources, including this book.

We come to writing with a natural working style. Some writers outline; others discover their ideas as they work through a first draft. Some writers produce small chunks, maybe 250 words a day. Others bang out massive swaths of text, producing thousands of words each week. Some people write in various forms and genres. Others pick a lane and stay in it.

Most writers want to make improvements to their working style. They want to write more or write faster or finish a project. They want to refine their habits. Even some of the most experienced and successful writers in the world want to cultivate better writing practices.

Ideally, your working style will align with your goals. Let's say you only write when you feel inspired. You sometimes go days or weeks without writing. Then you get an idea and write for a while until your inspiration wanes and you're back to not writing. But you've set a goal to complete a poetry collection of about a hundred poems, and you want to finish it within a year.

Your working style and your goals are not aligned, which means you'll need to change your habits or adjust your goals. You figure you can accomplish your goal if you write five days a week, regardless of how inspired you're feeling. Your other option is to change your goal and remove the self-imposed deadline, taking more than a year to complete the project, or perhaps never finishing it at all.

But wait—what if you don't have any writing goals? What if you're not concerned about your writing habits or working style? You just want to write creatively without any rules, restrictions, or impositions. That's fine too. If you write for pleasure or personal reasons, the best working style for you might be whatever is most comfortable or natural to you. You certainly don't need to set goals to enjoy creative writing and reap its benefits.

But if you do have goals and want to refine your working style, you'll likely do so by seeking out writing advice that points you toward your objective. And there's plenty of writing advice out there.

I've been blogging about writing for well over a decade, and I've doled out my share of writing advice. But I always try to issue a disclaimer: What works for one person might not work for another, and what works well for most people might not work for you. I believe in best practices, techniques and strategies that have been proven to work for many writers. But best practices don't work for everyone, and plenty of writers have succeeded despite forgoing conventional wisdom. When you come across writing advice, you can assess it, determine whether it aligns with your goals, and then decide whether to adopt it.

So as you navigate writing advice, be open to it, but always weigh it against your goals. Be willing to try different techniques, methods, and practices. If you can do that, you'll find writing habits and practices that work best for you.

Questions

What are your current writing habits and practices? Do you want to write more, write better, or write faster? What are your writing goals? What writing advice has helped you? Have you ever encountered bad writing advice? Was it bad advice, or was it just advice that didn't work for you?

4

Getting Started

We think about writing. We talk about writing. We have ideas. We have a plan: We know what we want to write and when we're going to write it. But when we sit down to do the work, sometimes a resistance rises up—something that prevents us from putting the first word on the page.

You might find yourself thinking of the great writers who came before—and who are alive right now, probably tapping out their next masterpieces. Who are you to throw your hat in the ring with such luminaries? Other times, you'll have a sense of what you want to write—maybe you can picture it or feel it—but you just can't put it into words. Every sentence that comes to your mind is trash. So you stare at your notebook— or your computer screen—waiting for something to happen, waiting for a marvelous—or even decent—sentence to appear. Tension creeps into your neck and shoulders. You clench your jaw and grit your teeth. Frustration sets in.

Your mind starts to wander. You need to pay the bills. The laundry is piling up. You've been meaning to call an old friend. Your inbox is full of emails that you need to answer. You can't remember if you let the dog out this morning.

Suddenly, you remember what you're supposed to be doing. You turn your attention back to the blank page and stare at it with disgust. Maybe you should check your phone, clean the litter box. See a shrink. You're certain that whatever you put on that page will be utter garbage—a waste of time.

This happens to almost every writer I've ever known. Yet somehow, they all manage to eventually get their writing done.

Maybe you face this resistance every day when you're writing in your journal. Maybe it only happens when you start a new project. Maybe it's whenever you're about to draft a new chapter for your work in progress. It probably doesn't happen every time you write. Sometimes, you'll come up with the perfect sentence immediately, so you're off and running without hesitation as soon as your writing session begins. But other times, getting those first words out will be a test of your willpower.

Write the Garbage

Nobody wants to write badly, but we all do it. Sometimes, we just need to warm up. After a few paragraphs of questionable sentences, the words and ideas start to flow. Other times, your writing will be stilted for an entire session. With a little luck, the occasional sentence or random idea will be usable. And then there are the times when the material you produce ends up in the recycle bin.

What you need to remember is this: It's okay to write garbage. We all do it. You probably need to get it out of your system, so go ahead and get it over with. You can clean it up later, or you can throw it away.

Small Chunks

The blank page can be intimidating, and the longer you stare it, the more intimidating it becomes. How will you possibly fill up all that white space? Should you really be spending time on this right now? After all, there are other things you could be doing.

Forget about the page and focus on the first sentence, the first word. Allow yourself to write a bad sentence. A bad sentence is better than no sentence. So do it. Get that first sentence down, even if it's terrible. Take a breath and do it again. Write another sentence. Then another.

That's how we do it: one word, one thought, one sentence at a time.

If you can break your writing into smaller chunks, it will be easier to tackle. If you're trying to fill a page in your journal, all you need is a first sentence (don't worry about how good or bad it is—just write it). Are you writing an essay? Just get that first paragraph out. A book? Take it one scene or one chapter at a time. Working on a scene or chapter for your book? Just write that first paragraph, that first sentence.

Planning and Preparation

Outlining and warm-ups can make the blank page easier to face. Having some idea of what we want to write eases the tension.

Before writing a draft, I often create a bulleted outline that summarizes everything I want to include. This could be a list of points that I want to address in a blog post, or it could be a list of scenes for a novel. Other times, I brainstorm, which helps to get ideas flowing, and then all I need to worry about is putting those ideas into words.

Warm-ups work well when I'm at a loss for words. Sometimes when I'm getting ready to write a scene, I know what needs to happen, but I can't seem to form it into a clear narrative. My sentences are awkward, and I can't find the right language for what I want to convey. Often, a ten-minute warm-up (of writing garbage—see above) will bring all my words to the surface, and I soon find myself swimming in fairly decent sentences.

I usually know what I'm going to write each day, whether I'm journaling, writing fiction, crafting poems, or writing a book like the one you're reading now. I try to use my spare time throughout the day to think about what I'm going to write and how I'm going to write it. If I do this, then when I begin my writing session, I often have my starting sentence ready to go, which makes the blank page much easier to face.

Questions

Have you ever opened your notebook or sat at your computer, thinking you're ready to write, only to find yourself at a loss for words or ideas? Has it happened more than once? What do you think was the underlying cause of this resistance? Were you able to push past it and get your writing done? Will you force yourself to push past it the next time it happens? What planning and preparation can you do in order to prevent this in the future?

5

Freewriting

Freewriting, or stream-of-consciousness writing, is an excellent tool for daily writing practice and for creating material that you can later harvest for stories, poetry, and other creative works.

The concept is simple: You set a timer or choose a word count (or page count), and then you write whatever comes to mind for the duration that you've chosen. The idea is to let your ideas flow freely as you put words on the page. Nothing is too weird or bizarre. If your mind goes blank, you write the word *blank* over and over until the ideas start flowing again.

If you choose to time your freewrites, you might start with ten-minute sessions. After a few weeks, increase it to fifteen minutes. A few weeks later, go up to twenty. Twenty minutes tends to produce a decent writing session, but go longer if you want.

If you're writing on a computer with software that has a word counter, you might start with 250 words and then graduate to five hundred words, then 750, which is a good length for a writing session.

If you're writing longhand in a notebook, start with one page (if you have large handwriting or if you're writing in a small notebook, consider doubling it). Work your way up to two or three pages per session.

The more frequently you freewrite, the better you will get at it. You'll soon produce interesting passages of text, and if you freewrite every day, you'll develop a habit of writing regularly. Because freewriting is deeply creative, a lot of writers enjoy it, especially when it can be done in ten to twenty minutes a day.

But freewriting has other uses.

Foremost among these is creating raw material for use in other writing projects. Because language and imagery flow through freewriting, the practice often produces interesting ideas that work well in poetry. But freewriting can also produce raw material for stories or essays.

Through the process of freewriting, characters and worlds can emerge. Ideas, questions, and beliefs might surface. Anything from a premise for a novel to a thesis for an essay can appear during a freewriting session.

Freewriting is also useful as a warm-up exercise before a writing session. Many writers struggle to sit down and work on a project. Because freewriting is creative and enjoyable, it's a useful tool for turning on creativity to get words and ideas flowing.

Focused Freewriting

Usually in freewriting, we don't place any restrictions on our word flow. But the focused freewrite uses a guide, which can be a word, image, or idea.

If you're writing *blank* a lot, you can choose any word or image and freewrite about it. Let's say you choose *tree* for a focused freewrite. Anytime your mind goes blank, you return to the word *tree*. The image—the idea—of a tree guides your freewriting session.

You can use any word or image for a focused freewrite, and if you're struggling with writer's block during your freewrites, this can be a good way to get unblocked; eventually you can start freewriting without the guide word.

Focused freewriting can also be used to generate ideas. Let's say you're working on a story but you're having a hard time describing the setting. You can freewrite with an intention of describing your story world. The trick is to let your mind relax and produce whatever it wants—as long as it's related to this world that you're creating. Over a few days, you might freewrite ten pages of material. Later, you can review that material and look for ideas you can use in your story. You might find that most of it is unusable, but there could be a page or two of that will form the foundation of your story's setting.

Activity

Try freewriting every day for one week.

Time your freewriting session, starting at ten minutes. Increase to fifteen minutes about halfway through the week. If you'd prefer an alternative to a timed writing session, here are some options:

If you're writing longhand, write one page per day, minimum.

If you're writing on a computer, write 250 words per day, minimum.

Don't be surprised if your ideas start flowing just as you reach the end of your freewriting session. If you're feeling inspired and want to keep freewriting, then keep going for as long as you want.

Throughout the week, complete at least two general freewrites and two focused freewrites. At the end of the week, review the material you've created. Do any lines or phrases jump out at you? Highlight them! Were you able to produce material that could be used in another writing project, such as a poem, a story, or an essay? Harvest it!

Part II: What We Write

6

What We Write

Creative writing tends to focus on fiction and poetry. But there are many other types of creative writing that we can explore.

No matter what you write, it's good practice to occasionally dip your pen into other waters. It keeps your skills sharp and your writing fresh. Plus, it's nice to take a break from writing the same thing all the time.

Experimenting with different types of writing will help you accomplish two things: First, you might discover forms of writing that resonate with you. A storyteller who decides to study and write some poetry to enhance their language skills might fall in love with crafting verse and become a poet. Second, experimenting with different forms of writing will build your skills. A literary journalist who studies storytelling can craft articles that are more compelling by using story structure.

You're about to explore some common—and uncommon—types of creative writing. I encourage you to try them all, even if you just dabble.

Questions

What are some forms and genres of creative writing that you've written? Have you written a story or a poem? Have you written a personal essay (not as an assignment)? Have you ever kept a diary or a journal? What forms and genres would you like to try? Are you willing to try any type of writing at least once?

7

Journals

Journals are often confused for diaries. Technically, a diary is a type of journal, but a journal is any written log. You could keep a gratitude journal, a dream journal, or a goals journal. Many writers keep idea journals where they store ideas for current and future writing projects. And many keep general-purpose journals, in which they write anything and everything. Journals can also be used beyond the realm of writing; for example, you could keep an art, collage, or mixed-medium journal.

Journaling is a good way to build writing habits, especially if you can commit to doing it every day. Many writers spend inordinate amounts of time focused on editing, publishing, or marketing their work, which leaves little time for writing. A journal provides a place to develop and maintain a writing practice.

But a journal can also be a playground for creativity, a sacred place where we can experiment and explore our most personal thoughts and wildest ideas.

Journals are particularly useful for new writers because they provide an ideal space for exploring the craft of writing. You can use your journal to experiment with any type of writing, whether to enhance your skills or to try new ideas and forms.

Some writers maintain multiple journals: a tiny one to carry in a pocket or a purse, and a larger one kept on a nightstand or a desk. Some writers keep one journal for poetry and another for story ideas. Others keep a single all-purpose journal. Some journals are written in notebooks, and these can be cheap spiral-bound notebooks or fancy hardbound notebooks, and other journals are kept digitally.

I highly recommend journaling for all writers, especially young or new writers who are discovering their writing. At the very least, it's helpful to have a few notebooks or digital documents that you can use for journaling, even if you don't do it daily. After all, one thing every writer needs is a place to write, whether it's a text document on a computer or a composition book and a pen.

Questions

Have you ever kept a journal? What kind of journal was (is) it? If you were going to start a journal, what kind of journal would it be? Would you rather keep multiple single-purpose journals or a single all-purpose journal?

8

Diaries

A diary is a specific kind of journal in which you log the events of each day, resulting in a chronicle of your life.

Some people keep professional diaries as records of their work. Others keep personal diaries to record the events of their lives. Some diaries are legacies that will be passed on to family members. Others get published and gain historical significance because they capture the realities of a particular time and place or were kept by notable public figures.

For writers, diaries provide the same benefits as any other type of journal: daily writing practice and development of writing skills.

Diaries have other uses for writers. If you ever write a memoir or an autobiography, a diary will be a useful resource. A professional diary might one day provide fodder for a book about your field of expertise. A columnist might keep a diary in which they log their thoughts about various subjects and then refer to their diaries to compose weekly columns.

And for many writers, a diary is simply a place to think and express themselves, to work through their day-to-day experiences, however mundane or extraordinary.

You can purchase a hardcover diary with dates printed on the pages, which might encourage you to write every day. Some such diaries come with locks. Some say Diary on the cover. But you can just easily keep a diary in a spiral-bound notebook or in a text file on your computer.

If you decide to keep a diary, you will have to decide what level of commitment to make. Writing every day is ideal. But that's not realistic for everyone. Maybe you write in your diary five days a week, or maybe you only write in your diary when you experience something that you want to record. Or maybe you simply write in it when you feel like doing so.

Activity

Keep a diary for five days, and write at least one hundred to 250 words, describing the events of each day. What did you do? Who did you see or speak with? Did anything interesting or unusual happen? How did you feel throughout the day, and why?

When you've completed your diary trial, answer the following questions:

Were you able to write in your diary for five consecutive days, or did you skip days? If you skipped days, why did you skip them? Did you write about the same amount of words each day, or did you have more to say on some days? On average, how much (in word or page count) did you write each day?

Reread what you wrote. Did you learn anything about yourself or your life? Do you think you can use this material for some future writing project? Would you be interested in keeping a diary for the long term?

9

Letters

Most letters are written for the purpose of personal or professional communication. Some letter writers bring an artful flair to the craft, producing letters that are heartfelt or beautifully crafted. This art of letter writing is a long-standing tradition.

Letters that are prolific or profound might get published, particularly if composed by a public figure or for the purpose of historical preservation. People who enter the public sphere as celebrities or leaders will often get their letters published, including letters from long before they became famous. And the choice to publish personal or professional letters is not always up to the author—some of these letters are published post-mortem.

It's not unusual to find open letters published in newspapers. These are often written by public figures or organizations to address some cause or issue that they care about. These letters are addressed to a particular group or individual, but they are designed for public consumption, often to inform, persuade, or make a statement.

For writers who yearn to get their work published, it's often a struggle in the early years to find a path to publication. One way to get published if you're finding it hard to acquire clips and credits is to write letters to the editor of a news publication.

The practice of writing letters can build a variety of writing skills, starting with simple communication all the way through writing narrative in first-person point of view. Letters also have the capacity to be formal or casual, intimate or professional. And letter writing can be cathartic or therapeutic, especially if it helps you express your thoughts and feelings, even if you never intend to send a letter to its addressee.

Letter writing provides a vast landscape of options and opportunities to write creatively.

Activity

Over the next week or so, write at least three letters, choosing from the options below:

Write a personal, intimate letter to a loved one or someone who has hurt or angered you. Use the letter to express your feelings about this person, their actions, and your relationship with them.

Write an open letter to a public figure or organization, expressing your views and beliefs about them or their actions and behaviors.

Write a professional or formal letter. It could be a letter trying to land an interview or a job, or it could be a professional communication between colleagues.

Write a letter to an editor of a newspaper responding to a recent column, article, or op-ed.

Add a dash of fun to this activity by writing a fictional letter to a character you've created, and then invent an event or situation that you will discuss in your letter, or write a letter to someone from a book, movie, or television show.

Finally, decide whether you'll send any of the letters you've written.

10

Memoirs

Memoirs are personal accounts—true stories—based on narrow themes and specific topics. They are usually the length of novels or novellas; shorter works of this kind would be considered personal essays. Memoir topics focus on specific experiences rather than providing a broad life story (which would be a biography or autobiography). For example, one might write a travel or food memoir, which is an account of one's personal experiences through the lens of travel or food (or both).

Memoir is an accessible form of writing because it involves sharing one's personal experiences. While there might be some research involved, most content in a memoir comes from an author's firsthand experiences. Research might involve referring back to calendars or diaries, interviewing others who were present for events that appear in the memoir, and some topical research. For example, a memoir about traveling through the rainforest might include facts about the rainforest, which would come from research. But the primary focus would be on the author's experience in the rainforest.

Memoirs sometimes come under fire for containing inaccurate or misleading information. An author who misremembers events from the past might be forgiven, but intentionally fabricating details can do considerable damage to a memoirist's reputation and credibility.

Memoirs almost always include the author's family, friends, and other acquaintances, and this gives many would-be memoirists pause as they contemplate whether to put the people in their lives into the public sphere, especially when the details about them are salacious or embarrassing, or if they are simply private people.

But memoirs are popular with readers and can be therapeutic for authors to write. Memoirs about parenting a disabled child or life in the military are examples of uncommon experiences that people can share with others who are having those same experiences or who are curious about them. This is why memoir is both therapeutic and a gift to a broader community.

Memoirs also provide public records of an individual's account of events. For example, a director might write a memoir about getting a film made, or a politician might write a memoir about their public service. These memoirs can become useful research tools for the public, and they create a public record of historical people and events.

Activity

Choose an aspect of your life that would be suitable for a memoir. It should be based on a particular subject that you've experienced firsthand. Jot down some notes, do a little brainstorming, and craft an outline for your memoir. Write the introduction or the first few pages of the book, and then answer the questions below:

Would you ever write a memoir? Why or why not? If you wrote a memoir, what would it be about?

11

Essays

The word *essay* comes from the French word *essayer*, which means "to try" or "to attempt." An essay is a short format that usually presents an author's personal point of view and can include criticism, arguments, observations, recollections, and reflections around a particular topic.

Not all essays are creative, but plenty of essays flow from creative thinking. Some examples of creative works in the realm of essays include personal, descriptive, and persuasive essays.

Essay writing is an art unto itself. Some essays follow rigid rules of research and accuracy regarding facts and truth, but others are elegant personal accounts of an individual's experience or insights. An essay might set out to provide a detailed description of a person, place, or thing or offer an account of some event or experience. Another essay might attempt to persuade readers to a particular point of view or to take some kind of action, which could be political, faith-based, or in the realm of personal improvement.

There are guidelines for different types of essays. For example, most academic essays require a thesis statement. But most forms of essay writing provide plenty of room for creative exploration and expression, especially personal essays.

Because essays are so broad and can range from academic or analytic to deeply personal, there are plenty of options for writers to choose from. Let's look at a few types of essays that we can explore:

Narrative Essay: Narrative essays are similar to short stories, except they are nonfiction and usually relate to a core topic or theme. Such an essay usually makes a point or conveys a lesson using a story as an example.

Descriptive Essay: A descriptive essay avoids the author's personal thoughts and feelings and focuses on the who, what, where, when, why, and how. These essays are ideal for anyone who likes to examine a subject from every angle and for writers who enjoy composing objective, detailed, factual, and descriptive prose.

Personal Essay: A personal essay relates an author's thoughts or feelings on any given subject. Subject matter can range from food, health, and parenting to political or philosophical beliefs. The writer's personal experiences might be the basis for such an essay; however, personal experiences may be absent.

Reflective Essay: A reflective essay is about a personal experience and includes reflections on it.

Response Essay: A response essay is similar to a personal essay in that it relates the author's thoughts and feelings, except it speaks specifically about the author's reaction to something; books, movies, travels, and other events and experiences are all fair game.

Argumentative or Persuasive Essay: These essays present the author's position on an issue and apply logic, reason, and often, statistics and research, to back up the author's opinions. Such essays may also include hyperbole, fallacy, and other questionable or deceitful tactics. Persuasive essays are designed to convince readers to do something or see some issue from a particular perspective.

This is just a small sample of the various types of creative essays you can write. There are unlimited topics that you can explore.

Essays can also be useful within the context of larger projects. Let's say you're writing a science-fiction novel set in space and want to learn more about our solar system. You could write a descriptive essay about our solar system and start the project by conducting research that will be used both in your essay and in your story.

Activity

Write a four-page essay (about a thousand words).

If you shuddered at the thought of writing an essay because it sounds like a school assignment, you can relax. Essay writing can be creative, fun, and rewarding—not to mention nonacademic.

While academic essays are based on a thesis statement and structured to prove your thesis with supporting ideas and sources, there are other types of essays that are more relaxed, such as descriptive or personal essays. You can describe a person, place, or thing. You can share a story about a real event, written in narrative style. You can write about a personal experience that you've had or articulate your reflections on any subject. Write a persuasive essay or craft a response essay to a work of art or something that's happening in the news.

First, decide what kind of essay you'll write (personal, narrative, etc.). Then choose your subject matter. Here are a few questions to help you select a topic:

What are you most passionate about? What gets your blood boiling or makes you want to do a happy dance? Have you ever had an experience that fundamentally changed you or had a profound impact on you? What do you know a lot about? What do you want to learn more about?

Brainstorm some ideas. If necessary, do a little research. Then write a draft. Take your time by spreading this project out over a few days. Spend some time rewriting and editing, and then give it a final polish.

12

Literary Journalism

Traditionally, journalism is a straightforward, objective, and factual form of reporting on people and events. Today, journalists often infuse their writing with opinion and storytelling to make their pieces more compelling, to cultivate a more loyal fan base, and to persuade or even manipulate their audiences to a particular point of view. For better or worse, this new practice opens journalism to more creative approaches.

It's worth noting that professional journalism requires formal training to develop skills in interviewing, objectivity, and fact-based reporting. However, in the modern era, we've seen the emergence of citizen journalism, in which individuals without formal training report on people, places, or events and publish their findings and conclusions to a broad audience.

As consumers of news and information and as writers, we should all approach journalism with healthy skepticism and objective scrutiny, seeking out the best sources of information by checking credibility, authenticity, and legitimacy.

Literary journalism is a particular, modern form of journalism in which the writer carefully crafts language to share a factual story with an audience. For example, in a standard news report of a burglary, you are not likely to find a detailed description of the home that was burgled, other than some basic, essential details. But in literary journalism, you might get the kind of description that would normally be found in a novel, a description that brings the scene to life and pulls you into it.

Activity

Write a piece of traditional, citizen, or literary journalism. Start by choosing a person or event to write about. Then conduct some research and gather the facts that you need. Make sure to check and double-check your sources to ensure your information is correct.

Write a short piece of journalism (about five hundred words). It doesn't need to be in-depth reporting; you can report on a local bake sale or a friend's wedding.

As an alternative, write a fictional news article, but write about an established story world, such as your favorite book series or film franchise. Choose a moment or character from the story, and use that as the basis for your piece.

13

Poetry

Poetry is one of the most artistic and flexible forms of writing, allowing poets to create images with words, often abstract or with ambiguous meaning. A poem can be expressive, contemplative, or whimsical. It can cover just about any subject imaginable. It can be long or short—written in verse or prose, form or free verse.

Whether you're feeling sad, angry, or elated, it's therapeutic to mold your emotions into words. Even if we never share these poems, the experience of creating them is cathartic.

Through poetry, you can also learn more about yourself and your ideas. You might start to write a poem about one thing and find out what you really think about something else.

Poetry is concerned with the sound and musicality of language; therefore, writing poetry can feel like making music.

While poetry can be written at any length, it tends to be a shorter form of writing, making it ideal for busy writers and perfect for daily writing practice. A poem can be just a few words, as is the case with a haiku, which consists of three lines in which the first and third lines contain five syllables and the second line contains seven. Or consider the short free-verse poem "The Red Wheelbarrow" by William Carlos Williams, which consists of just sixteen words:

so much depends
upon

a red wheel
barrow

glazed with rain
water

beside the white
chickens.

If you've committed to writing every day, poetry can fit in your schedule, even if you're short on time.

But perhaps the greatest benefit of poetry is that through a bit of study, writers can learn a host of writing techniques, often in the form of literary devices. These literary devices are not exclusive to poetry, but they are easily learned through the vehicle of poetry, and they will deepen and enrich any writer's skills. Such devices include alliteration, onomatopoeia, and allusion, to name a few.

The study and practice of poetry naturally imparts writing skills that are useful in all forms of writing, especially with its emphasis on word choice, imagery, musicality, structure, flow, and economy of language. Put simply, engaging with poetry will make you a better writer in all other forms of writing.

Let's look at a few types of poetry:

Form poetry adheres to strict rules that guide various aspects of a poem, from number of lines, length and number of stanzas, meter, rhyme scheme, and more. Some common forms include haiku, sonnets, and pantoums.

Free-verse poetry is written in verse (lines and stanzas instead of sentences and paragraphs), but there are no structural rules or guidelines to follow.

Prose poetry is written in sentences and paragraphs rather than in lines and stanzas.

Some plays and stories are written in verse. Shakespeare is one of the world's foremost authors who wrote plays in verse, and Dr. Seuss was beloved for his rhyming children's stories. While these plays and stories aren't considered poems, they certainly borrow heavily from the craft of poetry.

But poetry is an undervalued art form. It's extremely difficult to make a living as a poet because there's not a substantial market for poetry. Plenty of poetry can be found online, free to read. This is great for the public, making poetry accessible to anyone who wants to consume it, but it means most poets can't earn a living from their craft. So poetry is often written for pure love of the art form.

Questions

How much poetry have you read? Which poems or poets do you like best? Have you written any poetry? What was the experience like? Did you enjoy it? Why or why not?

Activity

Try your hand at each type of poetry: form, free verse, and prose. Try to spend at least two days (or writing sessions) on each poem, starting with a draft and then using a second writing session to edit and polish your poem.

As you refine and polish your poems, consider the following questions:

Is every word necessary? Are you forcing words to fit some rhyme scheme, causing the language to sound unnatural? Is each word you've chosen the most precise and accurate word for what you're trying to say? Are you using plenty of imagery in your poems? When you read the poem aloud, how does it sound, not in terms of meaning but in terms of music? Does it have rhythm and a melody? Does it flow?

14

Song Lyrics

Close cousin of poetry, song lyrics are a fun and creative way to merge the craft of writing with the art of music. Writing lyrics is an excellent path for writers who can play an instrument or who want to collaborate with musicians.

We can explore and learn several elements of writing through the study of song lyrics and the practice of writing them. This form requires understanding of musicality (rhythm and meter), writing in form, and learning structure (most songs have a set number of verses and choruses with a bridge).

Because song lyrics are so similar to poetry, crafting song lyrics can be an entry point to poetry writing, or poetry writing can be an entry point into becoming a lyricist.

Many song lyrics have been referred to as poetic or even as poems. And some poems would lend themselves well to music. So what's the difference between poetry and song lyrics? Some would say that a poem can stand alone, without the music, whereas lyrics depend on the music to support them.

Activity

Choose a favorite song with lyrics. A simple song with a consistent beat, a steady rhythm, and a simple structure will work best the first time you do this activity. Write down (or print out) the song's lyrics, and make sure you have the song handy and ready to play (and pause).

Now write new lyrics to the song, keeping the original meter, rhyme scheme, and structure intact.

This is a fun activity to do over and over with different songs (it's also a great writing activity for kids). As you advance, try more complicated songs. You can also make up your own lyrics and music, especially if you can play an instrument. Or if you know a musician, set a date to collaborate and write a song together: you provide the lyrics, and your musician friend provides the music.

15

Scripts

As a writer, you can hit the screen or the stage by writing screenplays (for film), scripts (for plays), or teleplays (for TV). You can even write scripts for video games!

Scripts are designed for a visual medium (film, television, or theater) rather than a literary medium (books, magazines, etc.). Writing scripts can be useful for honing dialogue skills and for learning to visualize a story that you want to write.

As with a few other types of writing, scripts follow a very rigid format. If you ever decide to tackle scriptwriting on a serious or professional level, be sure to study the format and read a few scripts before showing yours around or trying to get it produced.

A script tends to strip away a lot of the excess in a story, revealing its bare bones through action and dialogue, with very little in the way of description or exposition. In the worlds of film, television, and theater, these details are left to the director. In fact, film, television, and theater are directors' mediums, which means the final execution of a script (or story) is the director's vision, although it might be based on a writer's original work.

Questions

What are your favorite films, television shows, theater productions, and video games? What interests you most—

writing a script for film, television, theater, or a video game? Have you ever read a script? Have you ever written one?

16
Storytelling and Fiction

Storytelling is probably the most popular type of creative writing. We often associate stories with novels, films, and television shows. But storytelling is used in every arena, from self-improvement to politics. Stories of all types are powerful because they offer a deep and meaningful way to connect with people and their experiences.

In the nonfiction realm, stories are firsthand or secondhand accounts of real people and events, which are written (or told) in a narrative style. Such storytelling is often found in memoirs and literary journalism as well as in sales and politics.

Fiction writing is the art of making up stories. Fictional forms include flash fiction, short stories, novellas, and full-length novels. These stories can be inspired by or based on real people or events.

Within fiction, there are countless genres. Some adhere to the realities of the world we all know, such as contemporary fiction, while a genre such as historical fiction explores the realities of the distant past. Other genres look beyond reality: Science fiction examines what's possible, whereas fantasy explores the furthest reaches of the human imagination. And horror examines our deepest fears while romance explores the ups and downs of love and relationships.

Fiction writing is a way to explore a universe of ideas ranging from futuristic technology or magic to the realities of life in the distant past, and most importantly, the human condition with all its confusion, complexity, and chaos.

Storytelling is a craft that requires writers to pay attention to many elements, from plot, character, setting, and theme to the very structure of a story, not to mention details like tense, point of view, and genre.

A well-crafted story makes storytelling look easy, as if anyone can do it with little to no training. Many an aspiring author has tackled a novel only to realize that writing stories is a lot harder than it looks. Yet it is a rewarding endeavor.

Fortunately, most elements of storytelling can be learned. Most writers possess a combination of strengths and weaknesses when it comes to storytelling. Maybe you're good at crafting characters but not so great at plotting. Perhaps you can concoct a captivating tale but have a hard time putting it into a narrative that reads smoothly. The good news is that you can leverage your strengths and work on your weaknesses through study and practice.

Questions

What are some of your favorite stories, including stories from your childhood? If you were to write stories, what form would you write? Scripts? Novels? Memoirs? What is your favorite genre in fiction? Have you ever written a story?

Activity

Write a story.

You can write a short story or draft the first chapter of a novel. You can craft an outline or create a one-page story summary. It can be a true story or a fictional one.

If you're not sure where to begin, use the tips below to help you get started and guide you through the process:

1. Many writers find that the best stories emerge when they start with a compelling character. Use the following questions to create a protagonist and induce a story: What does this character want? Why do they want it? What is standing in their way? What are the stakes?

2. Next, build a cast by surrounding your character with other characters, including an antagonist, which is someone (or something) that is preventing the protagonist from reaching their goal.

3. A lot of writers get lost as they attempt to structure a story. Using the three-act structure can help: The first act (about 25 percent) provides the story's setup (introducing the characters and story world and establishing the central story question or problem). The second act (about 50 percent) shows the characters working their way through various conflicts that result in some progress as well as some setbacks. The final act (about 25 percent) resolves the central story problem.

17

Speech Writing

Whether persuasive, inspirational, or informative, speech writing is a discipline that can lead to prosperous and interesting career opportunities in almost any field ranging from science to politics to education.

Speeches share a common trait with scripts and song lyrics, which is that the text is written to be heard rather than read; in this sense, speech writing is a performative category of writing.

Similar to certain types of essays, speeches are often designed to inspire the audience to some action or persuade them to a particular point of view. Speeches can also be journalistic, particularly if any segment of the speech contains fact-based information or if the speech is meant to educate people on some topic. But speeches can also be personal and packed with opinion.

Perhaps the most common place we encounter speeches is in the political realm, where candidates embark on tours to share their ideas with the electorate. But we also hear speeches at important milestone events, such as graduations and weddings. Some types of lectures, such as TED Talks, could be considered speeches, or close cousins of speeches. Sermons at churches, eulogies at funerals, and monologues within larger scripts are all similar to speeches, sharing the commonality of one person onstage speaking to an audience.

Questions

Have you ever heard a speech that moved you or persuaded you? What was it about? Have you ever written or delivered a speech? What was the experience like? If you wrote a speech, would you want to be the one to deliver it, or would you want someone else to deliver it? Why? What would your speech be about?

Activity

Write a short speech that will last five minutes. Start by choosing a topic, something you're knowledgeable or passionate about. Next, set an objective: Do you want to inform, persuade, or motivate your audience? Finally, write your speech. Be sure to time yourself as you read it aloud to make sure you hit the five-minute mark, and don't forget to revise, edit, and polish your speech.

18

What Will You Write?

As you venture forward in your creative writing journey, there is no shortage of works that you can create. You can write privately, or you can write material that is meant to be consumed by the public. You can use writing to express yourself, to explore and examine your ideas and experiences. You can use writing as an art form, as a tool to inform or persuade others, or simply to entertain. Writing can be a hobby or a profession.

Few other endeavors offer such a range of applications that can be practical—even essential—or whimsical, pure fancy.

And there's such a range of options to choose from: journals, essays, articles, letters, memoirs, poems, scripts, speeches, and stories.

The menu is big enough to satisfy any appetite. What will you put on your plate?

Activity

Choose a creative writing project that you've never attempted. Before you start, set some parameters for yourself. The goal is to experiment with something new. If you want to explore long-form writing, such a novel or memoir, set an objective to create a detailed outline, or write a first chapter. If you're going to try one of the shorter forms of writing, see it through to completion.

Repeat this activity as often as you can. Trying new forms will improve your skills, increase your knowledge about your craft, and it might even unearth a type of writing that you want to continue pursuing.

Part III: Tools of the Trade

19

Tools of the Trade

Writing is one of the most accessible hobbies you can pursue. All you need is a pen and some paper! Few arts and crafts have such an affordable entry point. Consider the cost of paints, brushes, and canvas or the price of a decent musical instrument. We writers are lucky. We can pick up a pen and a notebook for just a few dollars.

But there are plenty of other tools that we can acquire to make writing faster, easier, and more convenient. There are also resources that provide inspiration and help us strengthen our skills.

If our objective is to write seriously or professionally, then we'll need to invest in a variety of tools and resources. Many are optional. Some are not.

Beyond a pen and notebook, the most important tool for any writer is a computer. An electronic tablet will work, too, although you might want to get an accessory keyboard, as typing on a tablet screen is not comfortable for most people. We can also use smartphones to write electronically, but again, the small screen doesn't offer the best experience. A laptop or desktop computer with a full-sized keyboard will be optimal. Fortunately, most of us own or have access to a computer (if not, check with your local library; most libraries offer free computer use). You'll need a word-processing program for your computer, too.

These are the basics. Beyond a notebook, a pen, and a computer with some word-processing software installed, each writer has their own preferred tools and resources. Some use whiteboards for brainstorming; others use sticky notes. Some use productivity tools to improve focus during writing sessions; others can write in a busy café at lunch hour.

And of course, all manner of office supplies can come in handy, from paper clips to index cards. We also need to organize any work that we write longhand or print out, so binders and folders are good to have on hand.

It can get pretty elaborate. And when you first start writing you might feel like you need all these tools and supplies— immediately. But you don't. Acquiring a collection of tools, resources, and supplies will be helpful, but it's not absolutely necessary. Don't make the mistake of refusing to write because you don't have the perfect pen or the right binder. In other words: Don't make excuses. Do what you can with what you have (or what you can afford), and build your writer's tool kit over time.

Activity

Start a list of writing tools, resources, and supplies that interest you. Price the items you want to purchase, and figure out what will work with your budget. Make a plan to start acquiring the tools you want (or need) for your writing.

20

A Notebook and a Pen

These days, we writers use computers, electronic tablets, and even our smartphones for most of our creative writing. But a lot of us admit there's still something about good, old-fashioned pen and paper that really gets creativity flowing.

I've often said that one of the wonderful things about writing is that all you need to get started is a notebook and a pen.

It sounds so simple: a notebook and a pen.

But over the years, I've discovered that, like many things, it's not that simple. As soon as you start perusing notebooks and pens in a store, you'll realize that there are many to choose from, and it's hard to know which ones to pick.

It's not unusual for people to view writing as a sacred act, which can lead to coveting a fancy notebook and an expensive pen. But I've found that costly materials create a barrier. Many writers find that they are more resistant to writing—and in particular, they are resistant to writing freely—when working with tools that seem precious. It's almost as if a beautiful hardbound notebook with archival-quality paper should only be used for a masterpiece. It's not for scrawling and doodling, jotting down random notes and weird ideas.

As for the pen, I've yet to try an expensive pen that writes any better than some of the throwaway ball-point pens that I've used over the years. As with a fancy journal, we might want to reserve the precious ink in an expensive pen for a special project, which prevents us from creating freely.

When we create, it's important that we feel uninhibited. That doesn't mean we can't work within guidelines or limitations (as we do when writing form poetry). But if we're holding back ideas because we don't think they're good enough for the paper we're writing them on, something's not right.

If you can afford several notebooks and pens, by all means, include some fancy ones in your collection. But be sure to have basic tools that you're not afraid to get dirty.

Almost every writer I know has accumulated a large collection of notebooks and journals. But I recommend starting simple: Pick up a composition notebook or a spiral-bound notebook. I like a 5x7 spiral-bound with perforated pages and storage pockets for all-purpose writing and note taking.

Eventually, you might want to try fancier notebooks. Here's what I've found:

Moleskines are pricey but worth the cost. They come in hardbound and softbound, various sizes and colors, and lined or blank. These are quality notebooks with both high-end and affordable options. I keep a hardbound journal with archival-quality paper for freewriting, drafting poetry, and doodling. I've also found that I prefer blank pages, which allow me to include basic drawings and do some mind-mapping as a brainstorming method. But most writers probably prefer lined pages.

As you gain experience with writing, you'll figure out which tools you need and how to best use them to suit your purposes. You might need only one notebook at a time, using it for everything you write. Or you might want different notebooks for different purposes.

When choosing a pen, find one that writes smoothly and doesn't leave ink stains all over your fingers and blots all over the pages.

I like to keep a fairly large supply of pens on hand. I buy ballpoints by the box in several colors: basic black and blue for general writing; red for corrections; and a few highlighters for emphasis are my go-to pens. I also keep a supply of ballpoints in a variety of colors, which are fun to use when I'm working out ideas, especially when brainstorming and plotting.

For new writers, I recommend picking up a few different types of pens—nothing fancy or expensive—just pens that write well and comfortably. You'll know when you've found a pen that works for you, and then you can stick with it.

In this modern age of digital wonder, it's almost surprising anyone uses paper anymore. But in my experience, working on a computer or any other electronic device simply doesn't offer the same creative stimulation that good, old-fashioned paper and pens offer. And I've seen many writers say they have the same experience. Ideas seem to flow better when working on paper. I wonder if it's because writing longhand is a more tactile experience. Maybe there's something about engaging more of your senses that sparks the imagination. But I'm just speculating. We'd better leave it to the neuroscientists to figure out why writing by hand is often more engaging.

The point is this: A lot of people find that working with pen and paper produces more, and better, ideas. That's not to say we would want to write an entire book longhand. I'm a patient person, but I'm not that patient! However, I do use my notebooks for many writing activities, such as brainstorming, taking notes, freewriting, and drafting poetry.

Your experience might be different. It's possible that you'll sit down with a notebook in hand and only find frustration in its pages, whereas working with a keyboard provides a better workflow for you. Try both, and then use whatever tool works best.

Questions

Do you have a favorite type of notebook? What about a favorite type of pen? Do you find yourself drawn to various notebooks and journals? What does your ideal collection of notebooks and pens look like?

Word-Processing Software

Notebooks and pens can be a lot of fun, but writing a book by hand is a daunting prospect. The average novel is somewhere between sixty to a hundred thousand words. My writing hand cramps just thinking about it.

Throughout history, many authors wrote manuscripts by hand. But then along came the typewriter, and then the word processor, and finally, the computer, making the prospect of producing a book a lot more feasible.

From the printing press to the typewriter, technology continues to make the publishing industry more accessible—for writers, readers, editors, and publishers. Not to mention book distributors and sellers.

If you want to write for publication; if you want to write a long-form project, such as a book; or if you simply prefer working on a computer over writing with a notebook and a pen, you'll need some word-processing software installed.

We're going to get into the nuts and bolts of word processing, so it might get a little technical for a minute. But it's important to understand these tools and why they're useful for writers of all levels—from hobbyists to professionals.

Simple Text Editors and Basic Word Processors

All computers come with basic writing programs. PCs that run Windows have Notepad and WordPad preinstalled.

Notepad is a simple text editor, whereas WordPad is a word processor with some basic formatting options. Apple computers come with TextEdit installed, which is both a simple text editor and a basic word processor. If you're using another type of computer, check your user manual to see what kind of word processor comes with it.

You can get by with any of these programs, but only up to a point. Basic word-processing software will allow you to indent paragraphs, apply bold and italics, align your text, and set the font. These programs might also have grammar or spelling checkers and dictation capabilities, all of which are useful. But there are some key features that are not available in these programs.

Microsoft Word, the Industry Standard

The most widely used word-processing software is Microsoft Word, which is available for both the Mac and PC. You can also get it for your smart devices, and there's an online version that you can use for free, but it doesn't have all the features and functionality of a full installation on your computer.

Microsoft Word is the publishing industry's standard word processor, so if you intend to write professionally or submit your work to agents, editors, or publications, you'll need to use it.

Word is a fairly elaborate program with lots of features, some of which involve a pretty steep learning curve. If you think you'll need it at some point, get it as soon as possible so you can start learning how to use features such as Track Changes and Styles, both of which I highly recommend.

The Styles feature allows you to quickly and consistently format a document. For example, you can create a style called Chapter Titles. You can format the font, justification, spacing, and more. And then whenever you add a chapter title, you just apply the Chapter Title style and voila! Formatting is done. This becomes a huge time-saver and keeps your manuscripts looking good.

Track Changes is essential when working with professional editors (they all use it). When turned on, it tracks all revisions in a document, including who made the revision. You can then review the tracked changes and accept or reject them individually or collectively.

Additionally, many professionals in the writing industry will simply require that you submit your work as a Word document.

Apple's Pages

Apple's answer to Word is a program called Pages, which is very affordable (last time I checked, it was free), intuitive, and functional. It's far more robust than Apple's TextEdit, but it doesn't have the horsepower to match Word. Because it's not the industry standard, its use beyond creating and saving your own work is limited. But if you've got an Apple computer and want a solid word processor, this is a very good option when you're on a budget and don't need Word or can't get it yet. Like Word, Pages offers features similar to both Styles and Track Changes.

Scrivener: A Writer's Favorite Program

Scrivener is probably the most beloved word-processing program among writers. Microsoft Word might be the industry standard, but it was originally designed for business professionals. Scrivener, on the other hand, was built for writers. I wrote my first two books in Word and then switched to Scrivener, and I haven't looked back (although I do bring my manuscripts into Word for editing, I compose in Scrivener).

One of the most important features in Scrivener is the ability to create a project that contains multiple folders and documents. This allows you to see your entire project, in all its parts, on the screen, all at once. You can easily organize content by chapter and scene and quickly jump around inside any large project as well as move large sections of text with ease.

With Word, you can either save each chapter as a separate document, or keep all chapters in one long document. This makes finding a particular scene or sentence a hassle. You have to search or scroll through one or multiple documents to find what you need. Scrivener's folders and documents allow you to view, sort, and access different parts of your project quickly and easily. And once you get several chapters into a book-length project, this becomes essential.

Scrivener is also ideal for organizing notes, research, and other media—all within a single project file. A typical Scrivener file for one of my books contains folders for front matter, each chapter, and back matter, plus folders packed with notes, research, and sometimes graphs and images, plus old drafts and content that I've edited out of the project but want to save in case I change my mind and decide to use it.

Scrivener has many other benefits, such as a Compile feature that makes publishing e-books a breeze.

Each document within a project comes with a Synopsis card and a Notes panel. You can view your Synopsis cards on a corkboard to get an overview of your project. The Notes panel in each document is an excellent spot for jotting down reminders and questions that you want to follow up on later. I also use it to stash text that I've cut from a document until I'm certain I want to permanently delete it.

Although many writers these days favor Scrivener, Microsoft Word remains the industry standard. This means that the project eventually needs to be moved to Word when it's time for editing and publishing. But that, too, is fairly easy. Scrivener will export directly to Word, or you can copy and paste an entire project into a Word document with a few clicks.

Which Word Processor is Right for You?

If you get serious about writing, you might end up with all of these programs. But when you're just starting out, or if you only want to enjoy writing as a hobby, you can probably get by with a basic word processor, such as those that come with your computer. If and when you reach the point where you want to share your writing with others or get it published, you'll want to level up to Word. And if you want a program to make writing large projects smoother, take a look at Scrivener (it's reasonably priced).

Friendly reminder: Regardless of which word processor you use, set up a backup system so you don't lose your writing. Also, if you get stuck or confused while learning how to use any of these word processors, check the web, which is packed with free tutorials that show you how to use every feature imaginable (be sure to get tutorials for your software version and platform).

Questions

Which word-processing applications have you used? Which ones do you own or have access to? Are there any that you'd like to try? How do you feel about learning all the functionalities of a new word-processing program?

22

Tools for Getting Creative

I've yet to meet a writer who doesn't have an affinity for office supplies. We seem to be drawn to paper clips and pencil boxes, binders and sticky notes. If you write a short story and print it out, you'll need to use a paper clip or stapler to keep the pages together. And if it's a full-length manuscript, you'll need binder clips or perhaps binder rings to hold the pages. If you write with a pen, correction fluid is often useful. But which tools can actually be used in conjunction with creativity? And how can these tools boost or bust our creativity?

There are many ways to capture and organize your ideas in writing. If you have a good idea, you should write it down so you don't forget about it. But all those ideas can pile up. You might find yourself searching through notes, trying to find an idea you had months ago, which you want to use now. You might kick yourself for failing to write down the details of an idea that you've now forgotten.

Fortunately, there are plenty of tools for exploring and capturing your creative ideas. All you have to do is find the tools that work for you and develop a system that you can comfortably use for generating and organizing your writing ideas.

Getting Creative

Creativity often begins with brainstorming and sketching ideas until they're refined enough for a draft. You can brainstorm on paper or on a computer, but I've found a bunch of other tools that make brainstorming and project planning fun and smooth. Here are some of my favorites:

Index cards: Simple and practical for capturing ideas randomly or during a brainstorming session, index cards are compact and easy to carry around. They also allow you to spread out your ideas and view them all at once. You can rearrange the cards, group them in stacks, or shuffle them around. Index cards are ideal for summarizing scenes and chapters and putting them in chronological or logical order. Coupled with some highlighters or colored pens, index cards are one of my favorite tools for the early stages of planning a book-length project.

Magnetic whiteboard: This is another of my favorite creativity tools. A magnetic whiteboard is incredibly flexible. You can display and organize ideas that are written on paper and attach them to the board with magnets and then use colored dry-erase markers to make notes or draw connections between ideas. I often use my whiteboard and index cards for brainstorming, and I just snap a photo of it when I'm ready to erase it.

Let's say you're writing a novel. You've worked out the basic story line, and you want to get an overview of how the plot will flow. You can write summaries of the chapters or scenes on index cards and then attach them to a large magnetic whiteboard. Now you've got a map of your story. You can see all of it right in front of you. And if one of the scenes doesn't feel right, you can take that index card down and make a note on the whiteboard with a dry-erase marker. It's an excellent way to plan a big project.

Sticky notes: I prefer index cards to sticky notes because I can stack and store them, but sticky notes work well with brainstorming, mind mapping, and capturing random ideas, which you can stick to your desk, wall, or bulletin board for later use. They're perfect for jotting down quick notes or ideas that you want to attach to a page in a notebook or a scene summarized on an index card. I often use small sticky notes, flipped upside down, as bookmarks in my notebooks (or in paperbacks). This allows me to include a quick note on the sticky note, reminding me why I've marked that page.

Audio recordings and dictation: Several times, I've found myself full of great ideas while driving. I used to call myself and leave a voice mail, but now I use an audio recording app that came with my smartphone. Your computer and smartphone probably have recording capabilities built right in, and most computers also take dictation, using automation to transcribe your spoken words into text.

Stocking Up on Supplies

I like to get my supplies in various colors. With colored dry-erase pens, index cards, and sticky notes, you can color-code your project. You might want to use different colors for different settings within a story, or you might want to assign each character their own color.

Some of these items can be costly, such as a massive magnetic whiteboard. And while the rest are fairly affordable, the price tags add up if you try to get them all at once. If you're on a budget, you can get an item or two whenever you can spare the cash. But don't put off your writing because you're waiting to get your hands on some sticky notes or dry-erase pens. Make do with what you have until you can get the rest. The most important thing is that you get your writing done.

Questions

Have you found any tools that boost or hinder your creativity? Which tools have you used or would want to try for generating ideas and brainstorming? How would they suit your needs?

23

Supplies for Staying Organized

For years, I struggled with organizing my writing. As I experimented with each organizational method, I would figure out what worked and didn't work. I tried everything from hanging file folders to plastic bins and finally landed on binders.

The reason is simple: You can get a bunch of accessories for binders that make them quite flexible for storing writing projects. I keep all my printed or handwritten work—except for what's still in my notebooks and journals—in binders.

You might use a slim binder for storing ideas and a thick one for manuscripts. Or maybe you use one big binder for everything and then move projects out into smaller binders when you're actively working on them.

Organizing is easy with tabbed dividers. Whether you're using them to separate ideas, notes, chapters, and scenes or to set apart entire projects, you can use dividers to make it easy to find whatever you're looking for.

The pages go in and out easily by opening the rings. As long as you have a three-hole punch, you can easily add, remove, and move content around within your binders.

There are a host of binder accessories available, from bags that hold pens and pencils to folders that you can clip in for holding pages that aren't hole-punched.

Clear-cover binders can be customized with spine and cover inserts, so you can label a binder before placing it on a shelf, and you'll never need to wonder what is stored within it.

But binders aren't for everyone. You might find that a system of hanging file folders works better for you. You can also get boxes and bins of all sizes. I've even seen writers store their materials in baskets or backpacks! Some writers don't mind disorganization, and that's fine, too. But I like to know where everything is so I can easily find what I need when I need it—and you never know when you're going to want to pull out some project you started years ago that you've been thinking about revisiting.

Electronic Organization

These days, most of my writing is stored digitally. Computers come with a search function, so if you lose something, there's a good chance you can find it. But it's even better if you know where everything is. The short time you spend now creating directories and subdirectories on your computer will save you a lot of time later when you want to find a particular draft or an old poem.

I keep a special folder on my computer labeled WRITING. Within it, I have created many subfolders: Craft of Writing, Templates and Worksheets, Research, Freewrites, Fiction, Poetry, and more. Within these subdirectories, there are more folders. For example, my Fiction folder contains additional folders for short stories and novels. I have folders for completed works and works in progress. Collectively, I've created hundreds of documents within these folders over the years.

Everything is pretty clear and simple, so I know where to find just about anything, and I know where to save any new file that I create.

A Few Tips for Organizing Your Writing

Plan ahead. Before setting up a new system to organize your writing, think about how you work and what you need. Consider how much written material and electronic material you need to organize and store. Then develop your system, and give yourself plenty of time to set it up correctly.

Start small. Don't invest too much time, energy, or money into an organizational system until you're sure it will work for you. In other words, don't go out and buy ten binders, twenty packs of tabbed dividers, and a fancy three-hole punch. Get some basics, use the system for a while, and if it works, expand it.

Transfer to digital. I've found that digital files are much easier to use and maintain. They are searchable. It's easy to move files around. And they don't take up a lot of space in your house. They can also be backed up, and it's easy to store a second backup off-site. So it can be worthwhile to digitize some of your old writing, even if it means spending time typing it up, scanning it, or photographing it. There are even professional services that will digitize your material for a fee.

Let it go! Don't be afraid to purge old stuff that you don't need and will never use. Some writers cling to every word they've written. Be discerning. Do you really need all six drafts of your first novel, which you never intend to publish? Perhaps you could keep two drafts and shred the rest. This goes for digital and print copies.

Don't throw it away. Although you don't need to cling to every single word you've ever written, you don't need to throw it all away, either. As you get organized, you might be tempted to toss some of your work. It's one thing to get rid of an old draft when there are ten variations of it. It's another to toss out the only copy of a poem you wrote when you were a kid. I have heard of writers who get frustrated or annoyed and throw away their hard work only to regret it later.

Maintenance is crucial. Your organizational system will be useless if you don't maintain it. Stop saving everything to your desktop and start taking a few seconds (yes, it's just seconds!) to save your files into the appropriate directories or sort them into the right binders.

The more you write, the more papers and notebooks and binders and files you will accumulate. How organized you are will depend on several factors: How organized are you in general? How important is it that you can find what you need when you need it? How much time do you want to spend searching through your stuff to find a particular item? It might be that simply keeping all your writing in a big plastic bin or a single folder labeled Writing on your computer will work just fine for you.

Questions

Do you already have a system for organizing your writing? Is it working well for you? If you were to change your system or create a new one, how would you set it up? Will you maintain that system once you put it in place?

24

Writing Resources

To learn the craft of writing and develop our skills, we need resources. These can be as simple as a dictionary and thesaurus. But you might eventually need to stock up on more serious resources: style guides, books on the craft, and apps or websites that you can refer to.

I use a lot of writing resources, but there's no resource that I use more frequently than the thesaurus. I have a paperback thesaurus, but these days it mostly sits on a shelf. I constantly open a thesaurus on my computer's web browser, and I also have a thesaurus app on my phone. I remember the days before I had such convenient access to a thesaurus. I used to sit there, trying to come up with the perfect word—sometimes I'd make lists in search of the perfect word. Now it's just a few clicks away, and I couldn't be more grateful.

I've heard people say that if you need to get a word from the thesaurus, it's the wrong word. That's absurd. Sometimes the right word is on the tip of your tongue. Other times, your brain is busy with the substance of what you're writing. There are about a quarter of a million words in the English language. Don't expect your mind to have them all on hand at all times. The thesaurus is a tool. Use it.

I've never heard anyone say to avoid using a dictionary, and sometimes I wish more people would use a dictionary more frequently. If you're reading and you come across an unfamiliar word or a word whose meaning is uncertain or unknown to you, then take a moment to look it up. It will expand your vocabulary, which is the very foundation of all the tools you use as a writer.

Another resource that I have come to appreciate deeply is Wikipedia. I've been around long enough to remember hardcover encyclopedias, which often didn't include a subject I wanted to research, and articles in hardcover encyclopedias were always becoming outdated. In its early days, Wikipedia came under a lot of scrutiny because it's open source and wasn't considered totally credible. But Wikipedia's reputation has improved over time, and because all articles include sources, you can double-check the information you find there to make sure it's accurate. Mostly, I look up basic information, such as the scientific name of a tree or what year something was invented—simple facts that Wikipedia is just as likely to get right as any other resource.

As long as you have a computer (or other device with internet access), you can find resources galore, including name generators, free poetry, articles on the craft of writing, even online courses and forums for writers. Many of these online resources are free for you to use. Never before have writers had open and free access to so many useful tools and so much valuable information!

As you get deeper into the craft, you'll also discover all kinds of wonderful books that will help you on your journey. From general books about creativity to highly specialized books about specific elements of fiction to memoirs by authors (which are often packed with some of the best writing tips), you'll find a host of resources that will inspire you and guide your writing practices.

Online bookstores offer an excellent way to search for books on the craft. You can search for exactly what you need: character development, poetry forms, or essay collections.

Depending on your interests, you might also want to add classes or workshops to your resource collection. Whether you head off to a university to study creative writing, take a local workshop, or sign up for an online class, a little formal training can help you build community with other writers while developing your skills and cultivating good writing habits.

Questions

Which resources have you used while writing? Have you started a resource collection? What's in it? What would you like to add to it?

25
Writer's Tool Kit

A writer's tool kit includes all the tools we use to do our work. Some of our tools rest atop a desk, while others are tucked away in its drawers. Some tools sit on bookshelves, while others fit neatly in a purse or pocket. Some of our tools are used for a multitude of purposes beyond writing, such as our computers and smartphones.

Your writer's tool kit can be filled with anything from pens and notebooks to the sources you turn to when you need ideas and inspiration.

You'll probably find that when your tools are easily accessible, you're more likely to write. So find the best places to keep your tools, and then figure out which tools you need to add to your collection.

Activity

Start your writer's tool kit by finding places for your physical supplies that are easily accessible and within reach. For example, you might make a shortcut on your computer desktop to a folder where your writing is stored. Or you might clear some space on a shelf near your writing desk to keep a few of your favorite books on writing. Are your pen and notebook in a place that's easy to grab if you're struck with an idea?

Your writer's tool kit could be kept in and around a single desk somewhere in your home, or it could be scattered about. Your tool kit might be overflowing with tools and resources, or maybe you're a minimalist with only a few essential items.

Next, make a list of additional supplies that you'd like to add to your tool kit.

Don't let the absence of any particular items stop you from writing. Maybe you have big plans for a huge binder filled with tabbed dividers and pockets and pouches, but all you can afford right now is an old shoebox. Use what you have, but plan for the future.

Part IV: Getting Creative

26

Getting Creative

Sometimes, we're overwhelmed with writing inspiration. We work on multiple projects simultaneously and are constantly bombarded with ideas that we'll never have time to fully explore.

Other times, ideas are sparse, and none of them hold our attention or inspire enough passion to see a project through to completion. Some of our ideas get tossed aside because they're not original or interesting enough, or we get a good idea, but it arrives at an inopportune time, like when we're driving, showering, or otherwise engaged. And sometimes, there are no ideas at all. We want to write, but we're at a loss for inspiration.

Many of us cannot summon exciting ideas on command. We go about our lives, waiting for inspiration to magically appear instead of nurturing our creativity.

If you've ever struggled to find inspiration, you know how frustrating it can be when you want to write, but the words—the ideas—just won't come.

Creativity is fleeting, but we can cultivate it.

There are countless ways to keep inspiration flowing. Some creativity techniques are passive—we learn to view the world with open eyes so inspiration can get in. Other techniques are active—we intentionally engage our imaginations in order to spark ideas.

We all appreciate those magical moments when inspiration strikes, but those moments are rare. The rest of the time, we need to put a little effort into our creativity. Creative people from all walks of life—artists, musicians, and yes, writers—are often shocked to learn that creativity can be cultivated—that it should be cultivated and that we need to invest time and energy—not just into our craft but into the sheer act of being creative.

Fortunately, there are lots of ways to do that.

Questions

Do you have too many writing ideas or not enough? What do you do when you feel like writing but you're uninspired? Do you only write when you're inspired? Have you ever tried exercises that are designed to boost creativity? Do you have any favorite creativity techniques or activities?

27

Writing While Inspired

Sometimes, inspiration appears out of nowhere. You're taking a walk, and you're suddenly struck by the urge to write a poem. Or you're driving the car when you get a fantastic idea for a short story. If you're lucky, you're in a position to actually explore these ideas when they strike—you've got a notebook in your pocket or an audio recorder on your phone that you can use to capture these bursts of creativity.

But most of the time, we're not sitting around getting hit by the lightning rod of inspiration. We have to work at it.

There's nothing quite like that feeling of being inspired. It's a thrill, especially when you put pen to paper and something exciting happens—you produce a piece of work that you're proud of.

But sometimes, no matter how inspired you feel while writing, you revisit your work a few days later only to discover that it's not that great. Meanwhile, something you forced yourself to write when you weren't feeling inspired turned out to be quite impressive.

Writers experience this all the time. That feeling of burning inspiration often makes us think that our words are on fire and our writing will shine like a fiery comet. But it's often a misleading feeling.

Most of us get the best results when we work at writing and creativity. Ideally, we'll set aside some time to write every day—even if it's just a few minutes, and even if we don't feel like doing it.

I'm not going to try to convince you that writing when you're feeling uninspired is as exciting as writing when you're aglow with inspiration. It's less pleasant, more time consuming, and makes you feel like a struggling hack rather than the brilliant writer that you are.

However, you'll probably find that once you start writing and get warmed up, inspiration starts to flow. Creativity is like water—sometimes we just need to turn on the faucet.

Activity

Make a date with creativity. Choose at least three times over the next week when you will sit down and do some creative writing. Write these appointments on your calendar, or set reminders on your phone. Commit to these dates that you've set with yourself. Give yourself twenty minutes to an hour for each creative writing session, and decide what you'll work on in advance.

Before each session, rate how creative or inspired you're feeling on a scale from one to five (one being not very inspired and five being fully inspired). At the end of each session, give your level of creativity another rating.

When the week is done, examine your three pieces of writing. Do you notice a difference in your writing when you're feeling inspired compared to when you're not feeling inspired? How did your creativity ratings at the beginning of each session compare to the ratings you gave yourself at the end of each session? Did inspiration start to flow once you'd been writing for a few minutes, or was the entire session a slog?

28

Consuming Art

If we don't consume art, especially written works, on a regular basis, our creativity will dry up, and our writing will suffer. Art is food for the soul. It gives us perspective, stimulates our intellects, touches our emotions. It informs us. Art is understanding; it is knowledge.

But more importantly, it feeds our creativity. We can't produce creative works if we don't take them in. Writers should read what they write. If you write poetry, you should read poetry. If you write historical fiction, you should read historical fiction. If you write essays, you should read essays.

Consider a science-fiction writer who refuses to read sci-fi novels. Maybe this person doesn't like to read. Maybe they don't want other science-fiction works to influence their own. For whatever reason, they stay away from the genre. Let's say this person gets an idea for a story about a genetic biologist who figures out how to create dinosaurs from preserved DNA. Pretty soon, this author is on their way to recreating *Jurassic Park*. Won't they be astonished to learn that someone else already had that idea? Will they argue that their idea is original, assuring agents and publishers that they've never read or seen *Jurassic Park*? And how will that be received?

On the other hand, if this sci-fi writer is familiar with the genre, they could stick with their idea about creating dinosaurs from DNA but put it in a different context: Instead of a story about a dinosaur theme park, it's a story about dinosaurs escaping from a lab in a big city. Or maybe animal-rights activists discover the dinosaurs in a lab and set them free to wreak havoc on the city.

As with any industry, there are trends in writing and publishing. Vampire stories will surge in popularity. We'll see a swell of political poetry. Self-help books dominate the best-seller lists for a few years. And within any given genre, there are common elements and tropes—some of which should be fulfilled to meet readers' expectations and some of which should be avoided because the market is saturated with them.

If you want to put your work in front of an audience, you need to know your form and genre. And the only way to do that is to consume it.

But let's say you're writing for personal reasons, and getting published or acquiring readers is of no concern to you. Consuming art is still essential.

While reading or watching television, I have found story elements that would work in one of my projects. Sometimes, it's a simple plot device or storytelling technique. Other times, it's a setting, a name, or some detail, like an article of clothing.

Art, in all its forms, is also inspiring. Have you ever noticed that after watching an intoxicating film or listening to a mesmerizing piece of music you feel that creative impulse luring you to your keyboard or notebook?

When you make time to experience a little art or entertainment, you'll find that your creative juices start to flow. Not only will you enjoy yourself by having an entertaining and engaging experience, you'll also massage your creative muscles and come away with fresh writing inspiration for your own projects.

Creativity is contagious. The more you expose yourself to it, the more creative you'll become. The next time you find yourself floating around inside your own headspace when you should be forging your masterpiece, take a break to watch a movie, listen to an album, view some incredible artwork, or read a book, and let someone else's art inspire your own.

Activity

Give yourself one to two hours to immerse yourself in art. Here are some suggestions:

Watch a movie: It doesn't matter which genre or whether it's an award-winning film. It can be a film you've seen a dozen times. Pick a movie that speaks to you and leaves you feeling reawakened.

Read a book or even just a few chapters: Find a novel, book of poetry, or collection of essays that engages you. And if you find yourself reading something that isn't fully engaging, use it as motivation to try to write something better.

Peruse art and photography: You can go to a museum or check out the many art sites on the web. Sometimes, when I need a break from writing, I type something random or interesting into Google Images and spend a few minutes enjoying the beauty of art and imagery. It's good refreshment for the mind.

Listen to music: One of the best things about listening to music is that you can do it while you're doing other things, like exercising, driving, cleaning, or working on your creative writing projects. Then again, you can just lie back, relax, and let yourself get swept away by the sounds.

Dance: Not only will dancing get your blood pumping, it will increase your energy level. You'll be listening to music all the while, so this one's a double hitter with the added benefit of exercise!

When you're done, write at least one page about what you experienced and how it made you feel.

29

Originality

A lot of artists struggle with originality. Of course, we all want to be original, but is it possible? Is there anything new under the sun?

Some say there are no new stories, just remixed and rehashed versions of stories we're all familiar with. Often, when someone calls a piece of work original, a close examination reveals its roots in the creative works that preceded it.

Most of us writers have had ideas that we dismissed because we thought they were too similar to other works. But just because your idea is similar to another one, perhaps a famous one, should you give up on it?

Instead of giving up on a project that you think has been done before, you can simply make it your own.

Look at it this way: Everything already exists. The ideas, plots, characters, language, and subject matter—they're already out there in someone else's work. Originality isn't coming up with something new; it's using your imagination to put old concepts together in new ways.

To test this theory, see if you can guess the following famous story:

A young orphan who is being raised by his aunt and uncle receives a mysterious message from a nonhuman stranger. This message sets him on a new path, and he embarks on a great adventure. He receives special training from a mentor who teaches him superhuman skills. He acquires loyal allies, including a guy and a girl who end up falling for each other. Our hero eventually faces off against a terrible villain who is terrorizing everyone and everything that he knows and loves— the same villain who killed his parents.

If you guessed that this synopsis refers to Harry Potter, then you guessed right. But if you guessed that it was *Star Wars*, you're also right.

This shows how two stories that are extremely different from one another can share many similarities, including the basic plot structure and character relationships, and it proves that writing ideas will manifest in different ways when executed by different writers.

I'm not advocating for writers to go out and dissect popular stories and then rewrite them with a new twist (although that's not a bad idea). What I am advocating is seeing writing ideas through to completion instead of casting them aside because they have something in common with a story you've read or seen on film or television.

Creative writing is about imagination, discovery, and sharing your thoughts, ideas, and experiences with readers. I don't know about you, but I've had several writing ideas that seemed brilliant at first but later just seemed like a retelling of some old story that everyone already knew.

But when I read a superb novel or watch a fantastic movie, I often realize upon reflection that these works share elements with lots of other stories. I don't know if J.K. Rowling ever realized that Harry Potter had so much in common with Luke Skywalker. Whether she did or not, the lesson we can all take away is that she forged ahead and believed in the story that she wanted to tell.

Creativity isn't always coming up with something new; often, it's simply finding new connections, perspectives, and combinations of elements. Letting go of your ideals regarding originality and reshaping them with this new understanding will send you soaring into less inhibited and better writing experiences.

Questions

Do you ever discard writing ideas that you feel have been done before? Do you find yourself on a constant quest for a fresh idea? Why do you suppose some people have a deep need to produce work that is considered original? Have you ever examined a story or a poem that you thought was original only to realize that it shared similarities with stories and poems that came before?

Activity

Use the synopsis about *Star Wars* and Harry Potter above to write your own story (or outline).

30

Borrowed Inspiration

From epic romances to fantastical adventures, stories have been captivating audiences for centuries, and they have been inspiring writers (and other artists) for just as long. There is a longstanding tradition among storytellers of reimagining or expanding the greatest legends, myths, and fairy tales ever told, from the Greek classics to last summer's blockbuster films. And storytellers aren't the only ones. Poets have written responses, tributes, and criticisms of artists and their works throughout the literary canon.

One might say that art feeds artists.

Sometimes, this results in a derivative work, a piece of writing that is imitative instead of fresh. Derivative works are frowned upon. Reviews will often refer to such works as rip-offs and call the authors hacks who have done nothing more than steal someone else's work.

But you can also find some impressive and respectable written works that are purposefully and openly based on works that came before, and many of these writings are embraced, beloved, and achieve critical and commercial success, plus massive fan followings.

So when is it acceptable to use other people's writing as a foundation for your own? Why do some of these works get heavily criticized while others are widely celebrated?

Let's look at some common types of creative writing that are based on other people's work.

Fan Fiction

Fan fiction is a favorite pastime for hobby writers who are loyal fans to their favorite franchises. Google "fan fiction," and you'll find loads of stories set in the worlds of *Lord of the Rings*, *Star Wars*, *Star Trek*, Harry Potter, and *Twilight*—all critically and commercially successful science-fiction and fantasy franchises. But that's not all. Fans are also writing fiction based on the latest blockbusters, popular television shows, and favorite novels.

Some authors strictly prohibit writers from publishing material set in the worlds they've created (although they certainly can't stop you from writing stories in your notebook). They feel these works will negatively affect the integrity of their stories or compromise their brand in some way. Other creators either look the other way or encourage fans to play in their worlds.

Generally speaking, writing fan fiction might not be the best path to becoming a respectable or published author. The work is copyrighted by someone else, so you can't publish a book or short story and get paid for it (there may be some exceptions, as with contests or other programs by the few authors who are supportive of fan fiction). But fan fiction is actually a good training ground for young or new writers. It's an ideal place to practice storytelling: the basic elements are provided, so beginning writers can focus on the craft of writing.

On the other hand, maybe someday you'll be hired as an official writer for your favorite franchise (it happened to J.J.

Abrams, who got to write and direct *Star Wars: The Force Awakens*). A few authors might even invite a fan-fiction writer to include their work in a collection or cowrite a project with them.

The Public Domain

In their 1951 animated film, Disney combined elements from various stories and poems by Lewis Carroll to create the timeless classic *Alice in Wonderland*, which secured Alice a permanent place in our collective, cultural mythology. In 2010, Tim Burton brought us *Alice in Wonderland (3-D)*. This film told the story of a twenty-something Alice revisiting Wonderland, so it's essentially a sequel to Disney's original film.

This is basically fan fiction breeding fan fiction, but we categorize it differently because Lewis Carroll's works are in the public domain, which means anyone can take them and do whatever they want with them. You, too, can write an Alice story, publish it, and be safe from copyright infringement or intellectual property lawsuits as long as you don't tread on anyone else's version of Alice, which is protected under the law.

When we take our writing ideas from the public domain, the work is generally referred to not as fan fiction or derivative but as a reimagining, repurposing, or retelling.

Why are stories based on public domain works viewed and treated so differently from fan fiction? In these projects, writers are using material that is decades (or centuries) old, and the new work basically keeps the old work alive and makes it accessible to future generations.

Responsive Works

In 1899, Paul Laurence Dunbar published a poem titled "Sympathy," which ended on the line, "I know why the caged bird sings!" Seventy years later, Maya Angelou published a book using that line as its title, and later she published a poem titled "Caged Bird." Reading the two poems back to back, it's clear that Angelou's work builds on Dunbar's. Both poems—and Angelou's autobiography—are exceptional pieces of writing, and together they show how one author's work is built upon another's, and how it can be done effectively.

And this isn't a new practice. In 1599, Christopher Marlowe wrote the poem "The Passionate Shepherd to His Love," a seductive love poem that opens with the shepherd inviting his beloved to "Come live with me and be my love." In 1600, Sir Walter Raleigh wrote a response poem titled "The Nymph's Reply to the Shepherd," which offers a rejection of the shepherd's proposal, questioning his sincerity and arguing that his passion will fade soon enough. These two works offer a funny and clever exchange, masterfully crafted—after all, they're still around hundreds of years later.

All around us, there are works being written and rewritten, revised and reimagined, stretched and skewed, and used as inspiration for new works. Today, we have such easy access to reading material that it's almost impossible not to be influenced by our favorite stories and poems. Consciously or unconsciously, many of our writing ideas are borrowed from the writers who came before us.

Questions

Have you ever felt so inspired by another author's work that you wanted to write a response, tell a story in their world, or borrow some element of their writing and use it in your own? Did you do it? If you were going to write a retelling, a sequel, a reimagining, or a response, which work would you choose and why?

31

Curiosity and Creativity

Even though inspiration abounds all around us, we writers sometimes get stumped. We search for essay topics, plot ideas, and interesting language for our poems. Unfortunately, our searches don't always yield desirable results.

But by fostering curiosity, we can ensure a constant stream of creativity. Some of the best writing ideas come from asking simple questions: Who? What? Where? When? Why? How?

Most writers are curious by nature. We look at the world around us and wonder at it. Who are these people? What are we all doing here? Where are we heading? Why do we do the things we do? How will we move forward?

Remember how curious you were as a child? Everything you encountered spawned a series of questions because you were trying to learn and understand the world around you. Bring that childlike curiosity back, and you'll always have a full supply of inspiration.

It doesn't matter what form your writing takes or what genre you're writing in. By fostering curiosity, you can create a fountain of ideas.

Below are some questions you can use to get inspired. Mix them up, change them around, and come up with your own list of questions:

Who
>Who is this about?
>Who can help?
>Who is standing in the way?
>Who am I?

What
>What is the goal?
>What are the stakes?
>What is the underlying message?
>What if…?

Where
>Where did it all begin?
>Where have we been?
>Where should we go?
>Where does it end?

When
>When did it start?
>When did things change?
>When will things improve?
>When will it be too late?

Why
>Why did they do it?
>Why does it matter?
>Why take a risk?
>Why are we here?

How
>How did this happen?
>How does this make people feel?
>How does this sound?
>How will this get resolved?

If you can keep your curiosity on fire and continue coming up with new questions, you'll find that you can write your way into answers and constantly discover new writing ideas along the way.

As you work through your writing projects, you can also use questions to help you overcome hurdles that are preventing you from crossing the finish line. Not sure how to move a plot forward? Start asking questions. Don't know how to begin your next poem? Ask questions. Want to write a piece that is informative and entertaining? Ask away.

Throughout time, many great thinkers have used questions to prompt creative and critical thinking. Sometimes, one question will lead to the next, and you'll end up with more ideas than you thought possible. As long as you keep your curiosity well oiled and let those questions flow, you'll never be at a loss for inspiration.

Activity

Open one of your writing projects, and make a list of at least twenty questions that get to the heart of your project. Be sure to include a mix of who, what, where, when, why, and how.

As an alternative, try using any of the questions from this chapter as writing prompts. Simply place a question at the top of a page, and then start writing in response to the question.

32

Observation

When we open ourselves up to our surroundings and take in the details, we will find inspiration in the most unlikely of places.

Imagine that you're sitting in an airport, waiting to pick up a friend whose flight is delayed. It's been a long day, and you're tired, so you decide to rest in the lounge area and watch a movie. You put on your headphones and set your tablet on your lap. Soon, you're engrossed in the film, so you never see what's happening around you.

You don't notice two men wearing suits, who are standing outside of a café, having a heated argument. Passersby are staring. An officer is guarding an exit-only door. A woman flashes a badge at him and then disappears through the door. Behind you, a young couple stands up and walks toward the terminal, leaving a nondescript carry-on behind. An elderly lady calls after them and points to the carry-on, but they shake their heads and continue on their way. The elderly woman frowns and mutters, "I saw them set it down. I know it's theirs." At the airport gift shop, a delivery man drops a package on his foot, and two children perusing souvenirs point and laugh, but not at him. They're looking at something else.

There's a story, an essay, or a poem in there somewhere. But you missed it because you were plugged in. You weren't paying attention to your surroundings. You weren't being observant.

Whether it's noticing the way sunlight flickers through the auburn and golden leaves of a maple tree at high noon on an autumn day or the behavior of people in an airport, inspiration abounds all around you. If you're not paying attention, you'll miss it.

But if you are paying attention, you can absorb it, process it, and put it into your writing. That's the power of observation, and if you can cultivate it, you'll get some of your best ideas from taking in the world around you (and the people in it). Every day, you're exposed to bits of dialogue, interesting stories, and funny situations. Turn these into poems, stories, articles, and essays.

Activity

Set a date to complete this activity, or do it the next time you're out and about. Whether you're attending a party with friends or going to a store or just taking a walk around your neighborhood, make an effort to pay attention to everything around you. After your outing, write down every detail you can remember. Who was there? What did they look like? Who were they with? What were they wearing? What were they doing? What did they say? How did the place look? Was it bright or dim? Warm or cool? How did it smell? What sounds did you hear?

Write down your observations, recalling as many details as you can remember. Repeat this activity from time to time, and see if your observation skills improve.

33

Getting Out of Your Comfort Zone

Have you ever wondered what it would be like to explore a completely new form of writing? Are you willing to challenge yourself and get creative by trying something new?

Many writers specialize in a specific form, genre, or niche. Fiction writers are concerned with plot, character, and setting, and they focus on their genre, whether it's mystery, romance, or fantasy. Poets are consumed with form, language, musicality, and imagery. Essayists focus on the topics they write about.

Sure, some of us explore various types of writing, but how deeply are we willing to immerse ourselves into unfamiliar waters?

When novelists experiment with poetry, they are likely to improve their vocabulary, bring better imagery into their stories, and craft sentences with improved flow and rhythm. When poets experiment with essays, they learn how to approach their subjects from a different angle, broadening their perspectives. And when essayists try their hands at writing fiction, they learn how to bring the power of narrative into their work.

As an added bonus, working in different forms, even if only briefly, often rejuvenates your creativity, bringing new ideas to the forefront.

When we lodge ourselves inside a comfort zone, our work can become stale or feel formulaic, and our inspiration can dry up. That why it's beneficial to read and write a little bit of everything. That doesn't mean if you're passionate about science fiction that you have to start reading just as much poetry and nonfiction, and it doesn't mean if you're a poet that you have to divide your time equally between crafting poems and creating stories. But occasionally, you can take a little time to check out some other types of writing, both as a reader and as a writer.

Activity

Below, you'll find a few activities that will prompt you to explore unfamiliar territory in your writing. Choose a type of writing that you've never attempted before, or choose something you've only dabbled in. Pick a form or genre that you've struggled with in the past. Just pick something that you haven't mastered, and then dive in. It won't take long:

- Write a piece of flash fiction under a thousand words.
- Write a hundred-word poem.
- Write a thousand-word topical essay.
- Compose a newspaper column.
- Write three pages of a script.

If you're not ready to try a completely new form of writing, then expand within your preferred form. If you write horror stories, try writing a piece of contemporary fiction. If you write free-verse poetry, try writing a few form poems. If you write personal essays, try writing a response essay or a descriptive essay.

34

Drawing from Nature

You're on a walk, and you pick up a pretty leaf or an unusual rock and stare at it. Instead of taking it home and putting it on a shelf, you ask yourself some what-if questions: What if this isn't a rock, but a planet? What if this leaf were sentient?

Try lying under a starry night sky and letting your mind wander: What's out there? Who's out there? How far does it go?

You sit near a lake, a stream, or a pool of water and toss in a small pebble so you can watch the ripples dance across the surface. You begin to contemplate how one small action can have far-reaching consequences, good and bad. This gives you an idea for a poem or a story.

For many writers, nature has provided a boundless source of ideas and inspiration, from poems about the seasons and the stars to essays about the need to conserve natural resources to stories that take readers on grand adventures through forests, deserts, and the depths of the oceans.

Nature is all around us, in cramped backyards and sprawling forests. Even in the heart of a big city, we can observe a colony of ants marching across a sidewalk or watch birds from a rooftop. And if you find yourself far from nature, you can always go online and peruse images, videos, articles, and documentaries.

Nature is filled with wonder and mystery. Even just five minutes of immersion can spark your imagination and propel your writing.

Activity

Spend some time in nature. You can step into your backyard for a few minutes or head to a local park for about an hour. If you can't get to a place of nature, use the internet to peruse images or videos that depict the natural wonders of the world.

Then compose a piece of writing that is inspired by nature. Here are some ideas to get you started:

- Write a poem focused on some aspect of nature: a flower, an insect, a planet, a drop of water.

- Create a description for a natural setting that you could use in a story, or create a story premise that draws from nature.

- Craft a personal essay about an experience you've had with nature.

35

Harvesting Ideas from the News

During the Great Depression, hundreds of thousands of people migrated from the Dust Bowl to California and other western states. John Steinbeck told their story in his novel *The Grapes of Wrath*, which was developed from a series of articles that ran in the *San Francisco News* in 1936. But it was more than a story about people struggling with poverty in a downtrodden economic climate. Steinbeck's Pulitzer Prize-winning novel is a thoughtful commentary on injustice and the forces behind poverty. In today's news media, which is rampant with political, religious, and social commentary, one need not look far for writing ideas.

Open up a newspaper or magazine, turn on the news, watch a documentary, or surf over to your favorite news website. Guess what you'll find? Stories. Lots and lots of stories. And plenty of writing ideas that you can bring into poetry, essays, and other types of creative writing.

The news is full of colorful characters, from the lowliest criminal to the most glamorous business executive. Local heroes, big-time politicians, sports stars, and pop-culture celebrities all mingle together in the pages of your daily rag. Be sure to check the society pages and the obituaries, and let the people who populate these pages inspire your character creations. If you're looking for really far-out figures, try one of the tabloids or scandal sheets. You can turn the subjects of these profiles into characters in your fiction, or you can zero in on them as real individuals and write a piece of nonfiction—an essay, an article, or even a biography. You can write rant poems or tributary poems about them, or write poetry from their perspectives.

And if you're not in search of characters or people to write about, you'll find plenty more in the news, which is filled with all kinds of interesting plots for fiction and topics for poetry and nonfiction. Look to small-town papers for quaint stories that are usually overlooked by mainstream media. Large urban papers will carry national interest pieces. And many periodicals off the beaten path contain tales of the unusual, paranormal, and fantastical.

Don't forget about photos and other images. *National Geographic* or any travel magazine will give you a sense of setting and compelling imagery that can provoke a poem or a guided freewrite. You'll pick up interesting phrases like "down by the levee," or "at the railroad junction," that might spark an image, which in turn sparks a writing session. Or simply challenge yourself to write a detailed, descriptive essay about a captivating image.

Are you writing a period piece? The local library is stocked with archives of old newspapers and other publications that you can review and photocopy. Not only will you find creative writing ideas; you'll also pick up lingo and other details about the era. You might end up writing a poem about the Old West or an essay about a historical revolution.

When you want to sit down and write, don't wait for inspiration to strike. Make it happen. The news is jam-packed with creative writing ideas, and all you need to do is season it with a little imagination—your next piece of writing will be simmering in no time.

Activity

Give yourself about forty minutes to peruse the news, and check at least three different sources to confirm the facts of the matter. Take notes so you can return to them later if necessary.

Next, make a list of writing projects that you could develop based on what you found in the news. If you're feeling compelled, start working on one of those ideas: write a story, craft a poem, or pen an essay.

36

Writer's Block

Some say writer's block is a myth, nothing more than an excuse. But that's not true. Writer's block is simply feeling like you're unable to write. And it happens to most of us at some point. Every writer has been there: staring at a blank screen, waiting for the words to arrive. But they don't come. Some time passes. You wait. But still, the words don't appear. You sit there feeling frustrated and uninspired.

That's writer's block. But it's not the only way writer's block manifests.

At times, writers certainly lose their inspiration, but we face plenty of other challenges that prevent us from writing. There's usually some underlying cause, often something that's easily remedied. If we can figure out what's preventing us from writing, we can fix the real problem.

Each of us requires a different set of conditions to be productive and creative. Some writers can trudge through a draft when they're tired while others will just stare at the blank page with an even blanker look on their faces.

If you're exhausted, hungry, grumpy, or dealing with a headache, you might find it impossible to write. Whether you face these kinds of ailments occasionally or on a regular basis, it's important to acknowledge the real problem and then look for a fix. That might mean taking a break so you can take care of yourself, whether you need a nap, a nice, hot meal, or treatment for a headache or some other ailment.

Our emotional state can also interfere with our writing. It's hard to concentrate when you're in a bad mood, stressed out, depressed, or angry. In cases of a bad mood, a little positive thinking might pull you out of it. You can also use relaxation techniques to calm your anger or alleviate your stress. It's normal to be depressed after any kind of loss or trauma, and these times may call for taking a hiatus from your creative work. If depression persists for more than a few weeks or months, it's important to see a doctor.

Sometimes, you just don't want to write (or do much else, either). There's a deadline looming, but the sun is shining and the beach is calling. You swore you'd finish this chapter today, but you'd rather lounge on the couch and binge-watch your favorite TV show. The problem isn't that you're blocked; you're just feeling (or being) lazy. There are writers out there who constantly use writer's block as an excuse for being lazy. This is common when writers get burned out and what they really need is either a break or a little motivation. Look for ways to get your energy levels up (eat healthy, nutritious meals and get plenty of exercise), and revisit your goals to recharge your motivation.

Sometimes, you'd rather do anything in the world other than work on your writing project. In fact, you'd rather surf the web, organize your closet, or schedule a dentist appointment. You might even be seduced by a brilliant new idea that's tempting you away from whatever you're supposed to be working on. The grass may look greener, but it's not. The only cure for procrastination and distraction is sheer willpower.

Occasionally, we writers will go out of our way to avoid a difficult writing challenge. It could be that we've gotten our characters into a sticky situation and can't get them out of it, or it could be a poem for which we just can't seem to find the right rhythm. You might know, deep down inside, that you have to scrap some of your work or make major revisions to get yourself unstuck. Maybe you need to do some (boring or tedious) research. So you avoid it altogether. Instead of procrastinating, push yourself to face these obstacles head-on. You can also skip ahead and work on some other part of your project. If you're truly stuck, then ask a friend to take a look and offer advice. Sometimes, someone else can see a solution where we can't because we're too close to our own work.

Sitting and staring at a blank page often increases tension and further hinders your creativity by reinforcing the blockage that you're experiencing. Try removing yourself from your writing for a short time and get that creative energy flowing again. Fifteen to thirty minutes ought to do it. Stretching and moving your body will bring on relaxation and relieve tension while increasing energy. Or do something that gets your mind completely off whatever you're working on by mentally diving in to something different for a while. But pay attention to the clock, and get back to your writing in a reasonable amount of time.

Prevention

You can stave off writer's block by simply taking care of yourself. Avoid too much sugar, caffeine, alcohol, and junk food. Eat lots of protein, fruits, and vegetables, and drink plenty of water. Get some exercise by taking your dog for a walk, or go through some simple stretches or yoga poses each day. Moving the body gets blood flowing, and when blood flows to the brain, you become more productive and more receptive to your creativity.

Meditation serves many purposes. It helps us focus, clears our minds, and promotes relaxation while minimizing stress, all of which are ideal for creative people. Even a brief five- or ten-minute meditation will ease tension.

Schedule time for rest and relaxation. Get plenty of sleep. Don't run yourself down, and keep your emotions in check by finding ways to be happy.

Being fit and healthy is one of the best ways to stay creative and achieve your goals. As a bonus, you'll also feel good.

You have to nurture your creativity, too. Feed your imagination by taking in some art and entertainment (try not to overdo it—the point is to recharge your creativity), and keep a journal for ideas that you can use when writer's block strikes.

If everything else is on a good track but you're still not feeling inspired or motivated to write, try some creative writing exercises or prompts to get yourself going in new directions.

And if procrastination or lack of discipline are the primary causes of your writer's block, you can use a reward system: get your work done, and then treat yourself to something special.

I've stumbled through writer's block many times over the years, and I've learned that whether I need to take better care of myself, push myself harder to get things done, or face up to an undesirable challenge, writer's block can be cured, and usually, it can be cured easily once you've determined the cause.

Questions

Do you believe in writer's block? Is it possible to become uninspired for no reason whatsoever? Have you ever felt blocked? Were you able to determine the cause? Did you find a way to break through the block? Which of the problems described above have you experienced? Which of these solutions would you be willing to try?

37

Look to the Pros

It happens to most artists from time to time: the absence of inspiration, writer's block, or a lack of good ideas. Yet there are creative people who seem to have overcome artistic roadblocks—authors who publish multiple novels every year, filmmakers who produce annual blockbusters, and musicians who are on the top-ten list week after week. They know how to stay inspired, but how do they do it? Have they tapped into some secret, endless stream of ideas?

I always say look to the source. When I see successful artists and innovators who are consistently producing creative work, I find myself wanting to learn more about where they get their inspiration. It makes sense that as a writer you would look first to other writers to find out how they keep their creativity flowing. So go ahead and do that. Read biographies of your favorite authors, and listen to interviews with writers to see where they got some of their best ideas. If you look hard enough (or listen closely enough), these writers will explain how to stay inspired.

But don't limit yourself to writers. Inspiration is similar across all the arts. So check in with folks from other disciplines too. And don't limit yourself to only those artists whose work you enjoy and appreciate. You might find that a movie director whose films you don't care for has a creativity technique that works perfectly for you.

Activity

Make a list of your favorite artists. Include at least three to five writers and a mix of musicians, filmmakers, and other creative people. Over the next week or so, check in with these artists by looking for interviews (YouTube is a great place to find interviews) to learn how these artists find inspiration. Better yet, find a profile in a magazine, pick up one of their biographies, or find a documentary about them. Don't forget to take notes!

38

People Power

There's no shortage of written works that were inspired by people—from a loved one who becomes the subject of a poem to high-profile public figures that end up in essays to complete strangers who make their way into fiction, writers often get ideas from the people they encounter—in person and in the media.

There are poems that celebrate and honor distinguished citizens and poems that rant about public figures who abuse their power. Through poetry, you can explore what it means to be human, to participate in relationships, and to be affected by the actions of others.

And of course, nonfiction works are often inspired by people. From profiles to biographies and essays, various individuals have provided fodder for written works of nonfiction. You can write a personal essay about one of your grandparents, craft a profile of your favorite artist, or pen an essay about a politician who inspires (or outrages) you.

It's been said that you shouldn't anger a writer—they might put you in one of their stories and make you a villain. I've been surprised to find that lots of people love the idea of being the basis for a fictional character—even if it's a big baddie. The people you've encountered throughout your life can provide the foundation for plenty of characters to populate your stories.

And there are plenty of people to draw from:

Friends: Everyone has a friend who has had some wild experiences or who leads an interesting, unconventional life.

Family: Who do you know better than your own family? What are their most noble traits? Biggest flaws? You've watched them evolve and change over the years, giving you a front-seat perspective on the kind of personal transformation that characters often undergo.

Neighbors: Why is their garage light always on? What's in that enormous shed in their backyard? And who's that strange visitor who's always stopping by? You watch them and wonder about them. Make up a story about them, or get to know them and maybe you'll end up with an essay.

Coworkers: You've befriended some of them, and there are others you'd like to see get fired. Few group dynamics are more interesting than those found in a work setting where people are forced to build relationships with others for the purpose of a common goal.

Strangers: Many writers enjoy people watching, and for good reason. An interesting or unusual stranger can often provide a burst of inspiration.

Public figures: There are those you admire and those you admonish. From rock stars to politicians, public figures put out a lot of material that you can study and use as inspiration. For example, I like to find photos of public figures and assign them to my characters to help me visualize them; it's a lot easier to craft a story when I can see the characters in my mind.

Groups and organizations: Whether the execs of a corrupt corporation or a virtuous group of activists trying to make the world a better place, groups and organizations can give you tons of ideas for writing projects.

And then there's you: Yes, you! You can draw from your own personality traits and life experiences as inspiration for a writing project, whether it's a poem about your hair, an essay about your earliest memory, or some traits you instill in a character.

A word of caution: When you put people you know into your writing, be cognizant of how it might affect them and how they might respond. You might upset someone you care about, especially someone who is private or who might not like to see their flaws on display, even in fiction. Also, be aware of laws (disclaimer: I am not a lawyer, and this is not legal advice) regarding libel that could be used against you if you depict someone negatively or incorrectly. This is why most works of fiction include a disclaimer stating that they are fictional and not based on real people or events.

Questions

Have you ever been inspired by a person and put them in a piece of writing? Who was it, and what did you write? Is there anyone in your life or any public figure that you would write a poem or essay about? Anyone you would turn into a character in a story?

39
Making Connections

Sometimes, you don't need a new idea—you just need to combine things in new and interesting ways.

The Hunger Games trilogy, written by Suzanne Collins, captured the hearts and minds of millions of young adult readers. The books were then made into films that turned the story into a cultural phenomenon. So how did she do it? Where did Collins get the idea for a dystopian, young adult novel set in a future where citizens are required to tune in to an annual reality show so they can watch teenagers fight to the death in an oversized arena?

In an interview, Suzanne Collins explained how the idea came to her: "One night, I was lying in bed, and I was channel surfing between reality TV programs and actual war coverage. On one channel, there's a group of young people competing...and on the next, there's a group of young people fighting in an actual war. I was really tired, and the lines between these stories started to blur in a very unsettling way. That's the moment when Katniss's story came to me."

Collins drew a creative connection between two seemingly disparate events—young people fighting in a war and young people competing on a reality show—and she combined them, forming the basis for her story world. This idea led her to create one of the most successful book series of recent times.

What if you combined the classic story of people getting stranded on a deserted island with an old fairy tale? What if you turned a murder mystery into an adventure set in a jungle?

Look at the world around you. There are unimaginable things happening everywhere. Some are horrific; others are bizarre. Some inspire hope; others bring about deep disappointment. What unexpected connections can you make? Suzanne Collins found her ideas on television. You can find ideas in books and movies, in the news, and even among the people you know.

Questions

Can you think of any other stories that seem to combine old ideas in new ways? What about stories that bring together two things that seem unrelated? What kinds of elements could you combine to come up with a fresh idea?

40

Prompts and Exercises

One of the fastest and easiest ways to get inspired and find good writing ideas is to use creative writing prompts and writing exercises.

Prompts, in particular, are designed to spark writing sessions. You can find prompts for specific forms of writing, such as poetry prompts or story starters, and you can also find general writing prompts.

Some prompts are images, often interesting or unusual photos. Others offer a bit of text, maybe the first few words for a poem or a situation that could spark a story. Some prompts suggest a topic to write about, while others provide a list of words to use in a piece of writing.

Writing exercises are also useful for sparking a writing session, with the added benefit of imparting skills. For example, a character-creation exercise might ask you to create a character based on their goals and struggles rather than on their looks or family background. A poetry exercise will ask you to use a specific literary device, such as a metaphor. Writing exercises are a good way to learn more about the craft of writing while getting ideas for writing.

You can use writing prompts and exercises when you want to write but aren't feeling motivated or inspired. They're also ideal for daily writing practice when you're not working on a long-term project, when you're between projects, or when you're immersed in a non-writing phase of a major project (like revisions).

Prompts and exercises might also spark ideas that you can use in a project you're already working on. For example, you might discover a character prompt that inspires you to add a new character to a story that you're developing, and it might be just what your story needed.

Finally, writing prompts and exercises are excellent resources when you want to try new forms, genres, and styles of writing.

Questions

Have you ever used writing prompts? What about writing exercises? Did you find them useful?

Activity

Start a collection of prompts and exercises, and then keep them handy in case you're ever struck with writer's block or at a loss for inspiration. They are a reliant way to get your pen moving. And that's what they're for—generating writing ideas. You can buy books of prompts or exercises, or just search for them online.

41

Your Idea Archive

One of the best ways to stay inspired is to simply remain open to new ideas. Whether you're chatting with a friend, surfing the web, or watching a movie, always be on the lookout for inspiration that you can use in your writing. You'll find an abundance of ideas whether you're actively looking for them or passively bumping into them. But even if you have a compelling idea, it might not sustain a story or a poem. You need a constant flow of inspiration.

But what if you're working on one project and get an idea for something else? Should you drop what you're doing to chase a newer, shinier idea?

Probably not. Writers who do this often find themselves in an endless chase, always starting projects and then abandoning them when a new idea comes along. The result? They never finishing anything.

But you probably don't want to lose or forget good ideas. So write them down, and save them. You'll end up with a repository of ideas that you can turn to when you're feeling uninspired or when you're ready to start a new project.

I used to jot down ideas on whatever was handy. Some of them went into my all-purpose journal. Others were scratched on sticky notes or index cards. Some were entered in new documents that I created on my computer. When I went to look for some idea that I'd had, I often couldn't remember where I'd put it. At one point, I had about a dozen different lists of potential character names: some were in notebooks, others were in project files, while more were stashed in electronic documents on my computer, and there was a sticky note on the wall by my desk with a few names scrawled on it.

I still have ideas stored in various locations, but I've been making an effort to keep things a little more organized. When I'm working on a story, I don't want to stop for an hour to look for all my lists of character names. It's a lot more practical to make sure ideas like those are available when I need them, all in one location, and without a lot of hassle.

So I put together an idea archive—a place where I can stash any ideas that I find interesting but that I'm not ready to pursue. And whenever I'm feeling uninspired, I can turn to my idea archive to get my creativity flowing.

Here are some suggestions for creating your very own idea archive:

Use a notebook: I use a notebook with dividers and pockets, which allows me to designate different sections for different types of ideas. One section might be for poetry, while another is for fiction. Or one section might be for plot ideas, while another is for characters. The pockets allow me to store ideas that I jotted down on scrap paper. I also try to keep sticky notes handy at all times; they're easy to stick into any notebook, allowing me to write down an idea when it occurs and stick it in my idea archive later.

Go digital: Digital idea archives are also useful, especially if you can use a system like a cloud service that's accessible from all your devices. This means when you have an idea, you can record it no matter where you are. And if you need an idea or some inspiration, you can access it no matter where you are as long as you have an internet connection. Some digital apps allow you to take notes offline and will sync up later. A few services that work well for digital archives include Dropbox, Evernote, and Apple's iCloud.

Box it up. Another option is to simply use some kind of box or basket and drop all your ideas into it. If you're out to dinner, you can write an idea on a napkin, and then it goes into the box when you get home. Keep a small notebook or a pack of index cards on hand so you have a place to write down ideas when they occur to you, and then you can put them in your idea box later. When you need a project idea, you can simply pull one, randomly, out of your archive.

Double up: You might want to use some combination of these methods. For example, I use both a paper notebook and an electronic folder on my computer that are both designated for ideas and inspiration.

Over time, you'll probably accumulate a lot of ideas for your archive. But many writers fill notebooks with ideas and never look back. Make sure you revisit your archive from time to time, especially when you're in search of inspiration.

Questions

Do you use an active or passive approach when searching for writing ideas? Where do you stash your ideas when you're not ready to work on them? Where do you turn when you want to write but you're feeling uninspired? Have you ever lost or forgotten an idea that you wanted to use for a writing project?

Activity

Think about situations that spark your creativity, and make sure you have a way to record your ideas in those situations, such as keeping a small notebook in your purse or installing a voice-recording app on your phone. Also, consider your working style and where you usually write; make sure your ideas are accessible from there.

Finally, create an idea archive for yourself. Make sure it's easy to access when you want to make a note of a new idea and when you need an idea for a writing session or project.

Part V: Doing the Work

42

Doing the Work

When you experience a burst of inspiration that leads to a satisfying writing session, the results are exhilarating. Whether you've gotten some thoughts and feelings off your chest, written a piece that you think might be publishable, or taken a giant step forward with your work in progress, you are likely to feel elated.

Maybe you came up with an exciting opening scene. Maybe you crafted a poem that makes you feel like a laureate. Maybe you put the finishing touches on an essay that you're certain will win hearts and minds.

Your words flowed. Sentences chimed. Ideas tumbled out with ease. It was not only enjoyable—it was fun; you had a good time.

But writing will not always be fun.

Sometimes, you won't feel like writing. This can last an hour, a day, a month, even years. Other times, you'll hit a point in your project that is anything but enjoyable. You'll slog through sentences and groan through revisions. And other times, whether the words flowed or not, the writing you produce will leave you feeling disappointed.

You might start to question whether you should have taken up writing in the first place: Maybe writing isn't for you.

Maybe it doesn't fit your schedule or lifestyle. Maybe there are other hobbies you'd rather pursue, other activities that you'll be better at doing. Maybe you don't have what it takes. Maybe writing is just too hard. Maybe it's a big waste of time.

Here's what you need to know: This happens to all of us. Every writer experiences doubts. Every writer questions their abilities. Every writer wonders whether a project is truly worthy of their time and energy. Every writer hits bumps in the road.

And for many writers, these challenges don't disappear with time and experience. These same misgivings are just as likely to arise while you're drafting your tenth novel as they are during your first.

The difference between a writer and a would-be writer is that writers understand and accept that everything in life has ups and downs. Whether it's a job, a hobby, or a relationship, there will be high points and low points.

Writers write through the low points. They figure out a way to work through the difficulties. They do the work.

Questions

Do you walk away from your writing when you're not in the mood or when you're not producing your best work? Have you ever pushed yourself to write even when you didn't feel like it or when the work was difficult? How do you respond when a piece of writing doesn't turn out the way you wanted?

43

First Drafts

Let's get something out of the way: First drafts are bad. Usually, they're worse than bad—they're terrible. But they're supposed to be terrible. That's why they're first. *First* implies that there's something to follow—another draft. A better draft.

Sometimes, you'll complete a first draft and it will need to be thrown out and rewritten from scratch. Your second attempt will be better. If you're lucky, you'll be able to salvage some of the material from your first draft. With a lot of cutting and rewriting, revising and editing, it can become a good piece of writing, but that will happen a few drafts later. Sometimes, it will be many drafts later.

Once you accept that your first drafts will be rubbish, you'll find it easier to start writing and keep writing. You'll be able to write through the bad stuff, which is, of course, how you get to the good stuff.

Nuggets of Gold

Let's say you spend several days writing a chapter for your novel. When you finish the first draft, you've got about twelve pages of text. You've been very productive! But the next day, when you review what you've written, you realize that it's awful. You needed one thing to happen in this chapter to move the story forward—and while you managed to pull that off, the execution was pathetic. The narrative is jumbled; the characters come across like a bunch of clones; the dialogue sounds forced and unnatural; the descriptions—well, you forgot to include any descriptions, so it will be impossible for readers to visualize what's happening.

As you go over the chapter a second time, just to make sure it's as awful as you suspect, you notice something: Buried in those twelve pages, there's a half-page passage that's not half bad. In fact, it's quite good. You managed to convey one character's motives in a clever and interesting way. She's relatable and sympathetic. Her dialogue is even funny. This is salvageable—this is something you can use. Half a page.

Writing is like mining; you need to dig through a lot of rock to get to the treasure. If you can learn to push yourself through the bad writing, you'll eventually produce some gems.

Why would you do this, you might wonder. Why would you write a dozen pages just to get a few usable paragraphs?

Well, sometimes that's just the way it happens. Sometimes, there's a good idea buried within a mountain of bad ideas, and you need to write your way through the muck before you can get to the gold.

I'm here to tell you that those little nuggets of good writing are worth it.

When Luck Strikes

Bad first drafts happen, but they don't happen all the time. Sometimes, you'll get lucky. You'll write a poem and nail it on the first try, or you'll draft an essay that only requires some light editing. Over the years, this has happened to me with a handful of poems and one chapter of a novel.

The novel was almost done. I had worked through a bunch

of rewrites, revisions, and edits. I was getting ready for a final proofreading. But something was wrong with the first chapter. It didn't hook the reader. Try as I might, I couldn't come up with a way to make it more interesting. I decided to do a little freewriting to see what might emerge. In less than an hour, I'd written a new first chapter. This didn't replace the original first chapter—it was a new addition to the story. The original first chapter worked much better as the second chapter. Not only did the new first chapter hook readers; it needed very little revising or editing. Every time I reread it, I was astonished at how clean it had come out as a first draft. By the way, the contents of that new chapter hadn't come from some idea that had been simmering in the back of my mind. It introduced a completely new character and subplot that had never occurred to me.

I can't explain how this happened, or why. I've written lots of chapters for many books, and that was the only time I got a clean chapter on the first try.

I don't expect it to ever happen again. When I write a first draft, I expect dreck. I expect a bunch of gnarly text that I'll have to toss out. I accept that I will probably have to rewrite the entire thing, probably more than once. If I get lucky and produce a good first draft, then I'll be pleasantly surprised.

First drafts can be daunting, but in the end, they are worth every moment of difficulty and frustration—worth every lousy, miserable, beautiful, glorious word, whether you keep those words or delete them.

Questions

What has been your experience with first drafts? Have you ever gotten lucky and produced a clean draft on your first try?

Do bad first drafts ever bring you down? Have you been able to turn a bad first draft into a polished final draft by rewriting, revising, and editing it?

44

What About Talent?

One of the biggest myths about writing is that talent is a prerequisite: You need it in order to succeed, and you need a lot of it. Some people believe that good writing is pure talent; you either have it or you don't.

This is simply not true.

Talent certainly helps, but it won't determine how much you write, how well you write, how people respond to your writing, or whether you'll succeed.

Writing requires a broad set of skills. We all learn how to read, and then we learn how to write our letters and construct sentences and paragraphs using grammar, spelling, and punctuation. While it's true that some people pick up these basic writing skills more easily than others, just about anyone can learn them.

Now let's consider the additional skills that writers need.

Storytelling requires a variety of skills, and while a writer might be talented at some elements of storytelling, they will need to build skills in other areas. For example, a storyteller might have a knack for creating vibrant characters, but that same storyteller might struggle at crafting a compelling plot. Another storyteller might have a talent for plotting but must learn how to construct scenes that form an engaging narrative.

The same applies to poetry and creative nonfiction. One poet might have a knack for stringing words together in interesting ways, but the result is a collection of lines and phrases rather than a coherent work of poetry. A nonfiction writer could be a natural at converting real-life stories into a narrative but struggles with writing detailed description or compelling dialogue.

Talent must be supplemented with skill, and skills are learned and developed. That's why creative writing is not an art—nor is it a skill. It's a craft: a combination of skill and artistry.

Talent is a booster. It helps, but hard work, commitment, self-discipline, and a willingness to learn are far more important. In fact, sometimes, those who earnestly and diligently study and practice the craft will surpass those born with loads of talent.

Questions

What assumptions have you made about talent and the arts? Do you think talent is necessary, optional, or helpful? What do you think is more important—talent or hard work?

45

Motivation

The more inspired you feel, the more motivated you will be to write. But there's a subtle difference between feeling inspired and being motivated. Inspiration is about ideas; motivation is about doing the work. You could lounge around for hours, daydreaming poems and stories—without ever putting a single word on paper.

I remember the first time I wrote a poem of my own volition. The experience was magical. I wanted to do it again and again. So that's exactly what I did. Then one day I didn't feel like writing. I wasn't in the mood. So I occupied myself with other activities. One day turned into a week, which stretched into a month. Eventually, I couldn't remember the last time I'd written anything.

I was under no obligation to write. I hadn't made a commitment to write—to myself or anyone else. It was something I did because I enjoyed it. So why should I do it if I didn't feel like doing it?

But the fact that I hadn't written in a long time *irritated* me. I found myself in a strange state of contradiction: Even though I wasn't in the mood to write, I wanted to get some writing done. I kept waiting, day after day, for the mood to strike. But it didn't—not until I sat down and forced myself to do the work.

Within minutes, my mood for writing was reignited. Apparently, I just needed to settle in to it and get warmed up. I hadn't lost interest in writing after all. I just needed some motivation.

Motivation is a close cousin to inspiration, and many of the same things that block inspiration also cause us to feel unmotivated: We're tired, lazy, not feeling well, hungry, moody, distracted, or stressed. But I've found that motivation is even harder to summon than inspiration. I can be full of inspiration but still lack the motivation to sit down and do my writing.

So how do you get motivated and stay motivated?

For starters, many of the things that bring about inspiration will also motivate you to write, especially reading and engaging with art. But getting motivated often requires pushing yourself harder.

Set Goals and Make Commitments

If you're the slightest bit goal oriented, then setting goals will be a major motivator for you. The sheer act of deciding what you want to accomplish with your writing—even if it's only finishing a poem or drafting a short story—and then mentally making a commitment will boost your motivation.

Small, measurable goals are especially helpful if you need to get motivated. Try making a list of tasks that you can complete in a few minutes each day.

If committing to your goals is not enough to motivate you, then committing to others might work better for you. You can find a writing partner or join a writer's group, and get the added benefit of receiving feedback on your writing. Or ask a friend or family member to hold you accountable. Speaking of accountability, a lot of people find that making a public commitment, often via a blog or social media, is highly motivating.

Prioritize

We often push our hobbies to the bottom of our priority list. We go through life hoping we'll have time at the end of each day to do a little writing. But by the time the dinner dishes are washed and put away, we're worn out. It's a lot easier to veg out on the couch than to sit at a desk, writing, especially if we work at a desk all day.

Our priorities tend to motivate us. Consider the importance that some people place on their favorite TV shows. They will not miss an episode. When an entire season drops, they block off a whole weekend on their calendar for the big binge. That's prioritizing! And it's very motivating.

If you make writing a priority and give it both prominence and importance in your daily routine, you'll find yourself more motivated to get your writing done.

Track and Reward

Lots of writers keep track of their productivity in order to keep themselves motivated or focused, especially when trying to develop good writing habits or reach specific goals, like finishing a book.

Tracking works wonderfully with goal setting. You could set a goal of writing at least 250 words per day, five days per week. Use a spreadsheet to track your progress, and reward yourself when you meet your weekly goal.

Interact with Other Writers

Creative people often feed off each other. Whether we're discussing our writing schedule, sharing details about our projects, or just talking about the craft, it's a lot easier to stay motivated when you're connected with others who share your interests and passions.

You can find writers in your community by taking a class or workshop, joining a writer's group, or looking for some kind of meetup where writers gather. Consider attending open mics for writers or even book-signing events. Conventions are another way to meet writers, and you can attend panels and lectures on the craft.

You'll find most of these opportunities replicated on the internet but with an even bigger pool of writers to connect with: online classes and workshops, online writers' groups, and even random writers on social media who are open to connecting with others.

Timing and Routines

Some writers find that they are most motivated in the morning. Others like to write at night.

Planning some time for writing and making it part of your daily or weekly schedule can have an enormous impact on how much writing you get done. It also cultivates a habit. Whether you do it first thing in the morning, at lunchtime, or in the evening hours, building writing into your regular routine might be the motivator you need.

Your Motivation

I've gotten the best results with a combination of these efforts. I tend to be most motivated when I've set a clear goal for myself. I then track that goal by breaking it into smaller steps and then monitoring my daily word count and checking off the milestones I've reached in my project. I add writing sessions to my daily schedule, giving them priority on my to-do list. I've also found that regularly reading books on the craft of writing keeps me motivated, so when I'm not feeling the urge to write, I often crack open one of these books and read a few pages to get myself fired up.

Some other combination of these actions might work better for you.

The best way to stay motivated is to figure out what compels you to get your writing done. Find the things that make you want to write and make them a regular part of your life. And when you combine your motivators with whatever inspires you, your entire experience of writing will be improved.

Questions

What motivates you to write? Do you write only when you're in the mood, or are you able to gin up motivation when you're not feeling it? Have you ever written even though you weren't feeling motivated? What happened?

46
Fun and Games

Most of us come to writing because we find it enjoyable. Some writers love language. Others revel in creating worlds and characters. Many get a kick out of the process—developing a project from inception to completion.

But almost all of us encounter some aspect of writing that's unpleasant. For some writers, it's one particular step in the process—they don't like writing first drafts, or they find rewrites to be tedious. For others, it's a certain project—a short story was more challenging than anticipated. Developing one project might be a breeze, while the next is like pulling teeth.

One of the things that makes writing so interesting is that each project offers a different experience. And most projects include some step that is difficult, even painstaking.

If you come to writing because it's fun, what do you do when it stops being fun or when it gets hard?

Some people just walk away.

I went through this cycle many times when I was a young writer. I would start a project, and when it got difficult or tedious, I'd let it fade in to the background. Eventually, I'd come back to writing, but the project I'd abandoned would remain incomplete. After this happened a few times, I realized that I wasn't finishing anything, and I was forced to ask myself whether I wanted to write purely for pleasure or if I wanted to actually finish anything.

Turns out, I wanted to see a project through to completion.

Next, I had to figure out why I hadn't been able to do that. I realized that I wasn't pushing myself through the difficulties of writing, and I was giving up whenever it wasn't fun anymore. I had this misconception that the entire process was supposed to be pleasurable. Once I rid myself of that notion, I accepted that writing isn't always easy or fun, and I learned that if you can push through the unpleasant parts of the work, you'll eventually get back to the good stuff.

Plus, finishing a project is a truly rewarding experience— worth every moment of tedious, difficult displeasure.

Questions

Is there a step in the writing process that you don't enjoy? Have you ever worked on a project that was unpleasant from beginning to end? Do you push through the hard parts, or are you inclined to give up? Would you rather complete projects that get difficult, or are you okay with walking away?

47

The Zone

Some artists will talk about "the zone," a state of mind in which concentration is absolute and intense. In this zen-like state, inspiration can reach an all-time high. In fact, in this state, creativity is the high.

The zone is a balanced state between relaxation and sharply focusing your attention on something. You can be highly productive when you're in the zone, and often, you'll produce good work due to your heightened level of concentration. As an added benefit, most people find it enjoyable.

You've probably experienced the zone before. It often occurs when we're immersed in a television show or movie, especially when binge-watching. Time disappears. Nothing exists except what's happening on the screen. You've given yourself over to it, totally.

But you're not being very productive when you're watching television.

Luckily, plenty of other activities can bring on the zone. It can happen when you're doing something you love, whether it's gardening or cooking. It can also happen when you're engaged in tedious work. As a teenager I did a lot of beadwork, making necklaces and bracelets and intricate beaded earrings. Other than getting lost in entertainment (especially books), that was probably the first time I experienced the zone. I could do beadwork for hours and hours, completely immersed in the activity. Suddenly I'd realize that it was four in the morning—I'd totally lost track of time. Later I found that I could get into the zone when I was building websites. More recently, yard work has brought on the zone.

And sometimes, writing gets me into the zone.

Often, when you get into the zone, it's by accident. You didn't set out to get into this deep state of intense concentration. You just had an activity or task to do, and when you came up for air, you realized you'd been detached from the world while deeply entrenched in whatever you were doing.

However, accidentally stumbling into the zone isn't the only way to get there. You can get yourself into the zone. Hopefully, your natural affinity for writing will occasionally pull you in to the zone. But other times, you've got to do a little work to get there.

If you can relax and clear your mind before you start your work, you're halfway there.

Meditation is probably the best way to relax and clear your mind. Even a short meditation is a good way to prepare for a writing session in the zone. Spend a few minutes sitting in a relaxed position, focusing on your breathing. Breathe slowly, slowly counting to eight for each inhale and each exhale. Observe the clutter of your mind, and then let it go. Most people need to meditate several times before getting the hang of it, and you can find tons of meditation resources that offer more detailed instructions on how to do it and various meditations that you can do.

There are a few other ways you can bring on the zone. Lying down and immersing yourself in a piece of music that helps you relax and forget all your troubles could do the trick. A simple writing warm-up exercise might help you slide into the zone. I often read before my nightly creative writing sessions, and although it doesn't always get me into the zone, it usually gets me to a mental state that is pretty close to the zone.

There are probably countless other ways for writers to get into the zone. What works for one writer might not work for you, and what works for you today might not work a year from now.

Maybe all you need is a couple of minutes to prepare for your writing session: Relax. Take some deep breaths. Roll your shoulders, and relax your upper body. Take more deep breaths as you start to think about what you're going to write, and let yourself enter the zone—or something close to it.

Questions

Have you ever experienced the zone? What were you doing at the time? What do you think caused you to slip into the zone? Have you ever been able to bring yourself into the zone intentionally?

48

Bad Writing

You know what sucks? Spending a lot of time on a piece of writing only to later realize that it's terrible.

You might write something and think it's one of your best works, only to revisit it a few days later and discover that it's wretched—truly awful—something you wouldn't even show your mom or best friend. Or maybe you know you're writing terribly even as your fingers are striking the keyboard. There's a little voice inside your head wondering why you even bother. You see it through, set it aside, and later review it, only to confirm your suspicions: it's destined for the recycle bin.

You might write something and think it's pretty great, so you publish it or share it with others, and it isn't until months or years later that you realize it's mediocre at best, but probably worse than that.

If you're lucky, it's nothing more than a few pages— maybe a poem you spent a couple of hours writing or the first few paragraphs of an essay. But it could also be an entire book—maybe even a project you spent well over a year working on.

Yeah, that really, really sucks. I know because it's happened to me. Bad writing: it happens to all writers.

Let me repeat this: It. Happens. To. All. Writers.

But there's a bright side.

Some bad writing is salvageable. With some editing and revising, you might be able to fix the problems and make it decent. This can be frustrating, tedious work. But it's doable, and often worth the effort.

Other times, you will produce a piece of writing that is beyond repair. You might have to let it go and chalk it up as a learning experience.

And there will be times when you produce bad writing, but there's something in it that's worth saving—some kernel of a poem or some skeleton of a plot.

After weeks of brainstorming, outlining, and careful preparation, I once spent several months writing the first draft of a novel. I was surprised to find that despite all my careful preparation and hard work, it was unusable. I read through it searching for some scene, some sentence that I could keep. But there were none.

So I filed that document away and went back to the drawing board. I used the same characters and a similar story line with a new narrative. And that became the foundational draft for the first novel that I published. It was a complete rewrite and a reimagining of my original vision.

I came away from that experience with the sense that the first draft was a necessary step in my process of completing a novel. It's almost like I had to purge all the atrocious writing and bad ideas before the good stuff could come to the surface.

Bad writing happens. Don't berate yourself or give up on your writing. Accept it. Embrace it. And let it pass. Learn from it. Set it aside and start over.

Questions

Have you ever written something you thought was good

but read it later and realized it was bad? Have you ever felt like you were writing poorly even as you were composing your words? Do you keep writing when you feel like it's not your best work? Have you ever rewritten a project from scratch?

49

Finding Time

You want to get some writing done. You even plan to get some writing done. But suddenly the day is over, and you haven't written a single word.

Ah well, maybe tomorrow.

Whether writing is a hobby or a career objective, you might find it difficult to find time for it.

These days, we're all crunched for time. You'd think technology would give us more time for personal and professional pursuits, but it seems to have the opposite effect. The world just keeps getting busier and busier. Even professional writers get caught up in paperwork and marketing and have to scramble to get the actual work of writing done.

Finding time for writing might seem like an impossibility, but if you know where to look, you'll find precious pockets of minutes and hours that you can use to your advantage. If you have a jam-packed schedule, you probably just need to be more flexible about when and where you write. Or maybe you need to reevaluate your priorities and reassess your schedule. With careful planning and better time management, you can make more time for your writing.

Here are some productivity tips that will help you write more, even if you have a busy schedule:

Write first thing every morning: Most people feel refreshed after a good night's rest (and a hot cup of coffee!), so there's no better time to get creative than in the a.m. Plenty of accomplished writers have done their work in the wee hours before dawn. This might cut into your beauty rest, but it's a small sacrifice to make. Get up thirty minutes to an hour earlier each day, and use that time to write. If you can get some writing done before you hop in the shower, your day will be off to a great start!

Schedule writing sessions: If you have a busy schedule and your life is controlled by your calendar, then plan your writing time. Even if you can only squeeze in twenty minutes per day, you'll see a dramatic increase in your output.

Give yourself a break: Squeezing writing time into breaks can help you increase your daily word count. Even a ten-minute writing binge during your lunch break could mean a huge breakthrough in your plot or that perfect, poetic line you've been looking for. Because some of our best writing ideas come when we're enmeshed in other activities, mini writing breaks scattered throughout the day can move your project along in small but significant steps.

Multitask and leverage technology: It's impossible for most of us to write while we're doing other things, but we can certainly plot and plan while we're cooking, showering, and commuting. While it's not technically writing, planning a project is an essential step in the writing process. You might even be able to capture some words by using a recording device and transcribing it later. Record while you clean the house, repair a piece of furniture, or work in the garden.

Make a trade: Sometimes in life, we have to make choices. Give up one of your TV shows, and use that time for a weekly writing session. Reconsider accepting every party invitation that you receive, and ask yourself if extracurricular activities like playing in a community softball league are more important than getting your writing done. Somewhere in your leisure time, it's likely you'll find something less important than writing. And when you find it, make the trade. Focus on your passion.

Balance the necessities: There are things we all need to do: clean, exercise, prepare and eat meals. But if you're spending ten hours a week cleaning the house, you can probably put up with a little extra dust and give two of those hours over to your writing practice. Make bigger meals, and serve leftovers a couple nights of week. Go to the gym five days instead of seven. You've just carved out a few hours for your writing.

Ask for help: If you have too much on your plate and simply cannot find time to write, try delegating tasks to friends, coworkers, and family members. This will free up time in your schedule that you can devote to writing.

Stay off the internet: Need I say more?

Questions

Do you struggle to find time to write? What could you change in your schedule to make more time for writing? How are you spending time that could be spent writing?

50

Habits

Not every writer strives to be a master writer. Some just want to get published or eke out a living. Others write for fun, to explore their ideas, or to chronicle their experiences. But most writers strive to write well, and the best way to do that is to develop good writing habits.

Writing comes more easily to those who are born with talent, drive, and a steady flow of inspiration, but even the most gifted writers have to work at the craft.

If you're constantly struggling with grammar, spelling, and punctuation, your writing will not flow smoothly or easily. You don't have to become an expert, but if you learn the basic mechanics of writing, you'll be able to focus on what you want to write, and you won't get distracted by wondering how to use a semicolon.

A lot of aspiring writers find themselves spending more time thinking and talking about writing than actually writing. Sitting in a chair and putting words on the page sounds a lot easier than it is. Distractions abound. Writers must learn how to combat procrastination, stay focused, and finish projects. Cultivating discipline and staying motivated helps us when we want to write but can't drum up the urge or when we are tempted to abandon our work before it's completed.

Similarly, we need to know how to keep ourselves inspired. You can be sitting at your desk, hands poised over the keyboard, totally prepared to get some writing done. But if you don't have an idea to start with—and if you don't know where to look for inspiration—you'll be sitting there like that for a long time.

Cultivating good habits will solve all these problems. Whether you write as a hobby or strive to become a pro, good habits will make writing easier and more pleasurable. Most importantly, good writing habits ensure that you get your work done—that you actually do some writing.

Below you'll find a list of beneficial writing habits that you can cultivate. Try introducing one habit into your routine every few months.

Frequent Reading

When you don't read, it shows in your writing. Grammar, spelling, and punctuation are a mess. But there are more subtle indications too. Sentences are awkward, stories lack cohesion, poetry is riddled with unnecessary words and phrases. No matter how much writing practice you've had (and no matter how much you revise), if you don't read, your writing will always be stuck at an amateur level.

Plus, reading will help you stay inspired and motivated. Nothing makes me want to write more than simply reading interesting works by other authors. Sometimes, a character in a story makes me want to write a story of my own. A turn of phrase in a poem makes me want to compose some poetry. Or a book on the craft of writing makes me want to grab my pen and crack open my notebook.

And if I don't read regularly, my writing habits begin to suffer.

So set aside some time to read. Read as much and as often as you can. You can read one book a month or read for an hour every night before bed. Get up early, and read articles and essays. Spend a few minutes every Sunday evening reading a poem. It will do wonders for your writing.

Regular Writing

You don't have to write every day, but you should get in a good, twenty-minute writing session at least five or six days a week. If you can write for a full hour, all the better.

While some writers get by on binging (writing profusely for short periods and then not writing at all for a while), consistency will help you develop good habits while strengthening your skills. Think of it this way: If you exercise for five hours every Saturday, you end up sore. By the following Saturday, your muscles have weakened again, so you have to start all over. On the other hand, if you exercise for thirty minutes a day, five days a week, you'll build up your muscles, the soreness will subside, and you'll get stronger and leaner.

Your writing practices are not unlike your diet and exercise habits. You'll get the best results if you start slow and develop a regular routine.

This doesn't mean you have to do the same thing every day. Sure, you might be working on a novel, but you can take breaks from it and use your writing time to compose poetry or essays. If you don't have a project in the works, then do some writing exercises or tackle some prompts. I have found blogging to be an excellent way to ensure that I write consistently (especially between projects).

So establish a writing schedule; you'll have better luck turning daily writing into a habit if you do it at the same time every day.

Continuous Learning

Sometimes when you're writing, you'll encounter a question about grammar, spelling, or punctuation. You might wonder whether you're allowed to end a sentence with a preposition, whether you're using a word correctly, or which punctuation mark to use between clauses. Other times, you'll struggle with a problem related to the form or genre you're writing. Maybe you can't get your characters' dialogue to sound natural, or perhaps you can't figure out why a poem isn't flowing well, or your essay could be rambling and lacking focus. Some questions will arise that have nothing to do with writing. If you're writing a book set in a faraway city, you might need to know the size of its population.

Get answers to the small questions when they arise: Pause your writing and look it up. If finding the answer to a question is going to take a while, make a note and set aside some time to do your research later.

Most importantly, continue learning the craft. Find articles and books that teach you new writing concepts and techniques or that offer fresh perspectives on the craft. As long as you keep learning, your writing will continue to improve.

Finish What You Start

Shiny new ideas are always tempting us away from our current projects, and one of the worst habits a writer can acquire is to never finish anything.

Even if you're writing for personal reasons and have no intention of sharing or publishing your work, you'll miss out on that sense of accomplishment, which comes from finishing a project.

So don't give in to temptation. Unless a project is absolutely going nowhere, wrap it up before you move on to the next one. Otherwise, you'll end up in a vicious cycle and have nothing to show for all the work you've done.

Polish Your Work

After investing a lot of time and effort into writing a first draft, it's tempting to send it to friends, agents, or editors. Maybe you're ready to move on to your next project. Maybe you're in a hurry to get feedback on your work. Maybe you just don't like rewriting and editing.

Most early drafts need considerable revision. It's been said that "writing is rewriting," and it's true: even the most successful, experienced authors need to work through several drafts of their work.

If you send a messy draft to your writing group, beta readers, or an editor for feedback, you're wasting their time and yours. They could focus their feedback on all the issues that you could have identified and fixed without their input, which means you're missing an opportunity to find and resolve deeper and more meaningful problems.

An editor can only find and fix so many mistakes in your writing. Editors might go over a piece of writing two or three times, but eventually they'll stop seeing the errors. No editor can be expected to catch every single mistake and typo—after all, they're only human. The more mistakes there are in your work when you hand it to an editor, the more there will be when they hand it back to you.

Here's a good rule of thumb: Don't ever show your work to anyone unless you've revised it three times: one major revision, one edit, and one final proof. Ideally, you'll go over your work until you can't find any issues to resolve. Nobody wants to see your typos—not even your mother and certainly not agents, editors, or readers (including beta readers).

Questions

How many of these writing habits do you practice regularly? Do you think your writing habits are good or bad? A mix? Which of these habits would you like to adopt?

51

Your Process

As you progress with your writing, you may start to notice that there are certain steps you repeat for similar projects. This is your writing process. It often goes something like this:

1. Brainstorm
2. Outline and research
3. Rough draft
4. Rewrite (repeat as needed)
5. Edit, proof, and polish

This is a good system—it absolutely works. But does it work for everyone?

I find that the writing process I use varies from project to project and depends on the level of difficulty, the length and scope of the project, and even my state of mind. If I'm feeling super creative, a blog post will come flying out of my head. If I'm tired, hungry, or unmotivated, or if the project is complicated, then it's a struggle; I have to work harder, and it takes longer. Brainstorming and outlining can help, and I often have to complete more revisions than usual.

I don't have one creative writing process. I have several. And I always use the one that's best suited for a particular project.

Some writers can pound out an article, a short story, or even a novel without any planning or outlining. Others need to follow a strict process, or they get lost and confused, tangled up in their own words.

For example, when I am involved in a nonfiction project, I find that brainstorming and outlining are essential. I need to organize my thoughts and make sure I cover the subject matter thoroughly. When I'm writing poetry, I just start writing and let the ideas flow. Fiction writing is a cycle of writing scenes and backstory and then brainstorming and outlining until I have enough material to get serious about a first draft. I've even used different processes for different projects. I wrote my first novel without a plan or outline, but the second one (which was the first one I ended up publishing) started with a detailed outline and other developmental materials, such as research and character sketches.

Creative writing processes are good. The reason our predecessors developed processes and shared them, along with a host of other writing practices, was to help us be more creative, encourage us to be more productive, and show us how to produce better writing. Common and proven techniques and strategies can be helpful, but it's our responsibility to know what works for us as individuals.

It is only by experimenting with a variety of writing processes that you will find the one that works best for you. Think about the process you're using, learn about processes that work for others, and then experiment until you find your best writing process.

Questions

What's your creative writing process? Do you have one? Have you ever tried a process (or even a step in a process, such as outlining) that someone else suggested? Are there any processes or steps that you think would make your writing better or improve your writing experience?

52

Your Writing Practice

Like all things, writing has its challenges.

Sometimes, you won't feel inspired to write. Other times, you'll have ideas, but you won't be motivated to write. Sometimes, writing will be fun. Other times, it will be tedious, boring, or difficult. There will be times when you review your writing and find it lacking. You'll struggle to find time to write. You'll get stuck in the middle of a project, in the middle of a paragraph, in the middle of a sentence.

But through all this, what matters most is your hunger for writing, for putting your words—your thoughts, ideas, feelings, and experiences—on the page. If you can maintain that hunger, your writing will continue to flourish despite the challenges and setbacks that you'll inevitably encounter.

It doesn't matter if you write for fun or because you're seeking a career in writing—you will develop some kind of writing practice. Maybe you only write a few times a year, or maybe you've set a goal to write every day. Maybe you start every writing session with a ten-minute warm-up by freewriting. Maybe you end each day by adding a few pages to your work in progress.

Your writing practice will determine what you write, how much writing you produce, and the quality of your writing.

And your practice is up to you. After all, it's your writing, and you get to decide.

Activity

This activity will help you figure out your goals so you can consider and refine your writing practice. You can revisit this activity regularly (about once a year works well) to reshape and refine your writing practice.

There are no right or wrong answers to any of these questions. Your goal might be to keep a travel journal and write in it only once a year after you take a vacation. Or maybe you want to complete a novel. Maybe you want to improve specific aspects of your writing. Be honest—perhaps brutally honest—as you form your answers.

1. What are your goals, as a writer?

2. What is your current writing practice? When do you write? How often do you write? How much (in words or pages) do you write? What do you write? Do you have any rituals, like warming up or reading before a writing session?

3. Is your current writing practice moving you closer to your goals? If not, what could you change?

Once you've answered these questions, choose one thing you can change about your writing practice, and start incorporating it into your routine. Give yourself at least six weeks to make it a habit.

Part VI: Keep Writing (Tips and Activities)

53

Keep Writing

Hopefully by now, you've created a writing space for yourself and started gathering your tools and resources. You've considered what you want to write, whether it's an occasional journal or an epic novel. You've learned what inspires and motivates you, and you've tried your hand at various types of writing. You've even set some goals.

Now all you have to do is keep it going.

As you continue to write, you will encounter your share of challenges and questions about the craft, and you'll probably want to continue strengthening your writing skills.

You'll write a sentence and wonder where the comma should go, or whether a comma is even warranted. You'll start drafting a story only to realize that you're not sure what makes a character realistic or sympathetic.

You'll find plenty of websites online that regularly publish helpful articles for writers at all skill levels. Subscribe to them. Save the articles that you want to revisit later. Use them to learn new techniques and to remind yourself of techniques you've already learned. You'll also find books and interviews that will help you in your journey, along with fellow writers who can offer support and share their experiences while helping you stay focused.

Continue adding to your collection of writing tools and resources. Keep trying new forms and genres. Make lists of projects you want to tackle. Always be on the lookout for ideas, and keep a close eye on your writing practice. Revisit your goals on occasion to see if you want to refine them and to assess your progress. Read as much as you can.

But most importantly, keep writing.

Questions

What are some of the best writing tips you've encountered? Have you ever tried a writing tool or technique that didn't work for you? What are some of your favorite writing activities? What will you do to make sure you keep writing?

54

Writing Tips to Take with You

As you continue your writing journey, you'll come across various bits of wisdom and advice. Some tips will help you, while others might not work for you. Many will take a while to sink in and become habitual.

The writing advice you encounter will run the gamut, addressing everything from grammar, spelling, and punctuation to carving out a path through the publishing world.

Sometimes, all this information can be overwhelming, especially when you're first starting out. But take it all in stride. Collect the advice that you need, when you need it, and set the rest aside for later. Be open to trying tips, techniques, and tools. If they don't work for you, move on and try something else.

Some All-Purpose Writing Tips

Here are some snippets of writing wisdom that have served me well over the years:

- Every word matters. Choose your language with care. It's worthwhile to spend a few minutes in search of the perfect word.

- Be yourself. If what you're writing holds no meaning for you, it will show in your work. Write with passion.

- Kill your darlings. Cut the excess. Sometimes, that means deleting a few words; other times, it means letting go of an entire chapter.

- Metaphors often bring clarity to complex ideas. Use them with discretion.

- Rewrite, revise, and edit your work.

- Put a little extra effort into the opening of any piece of writing. That's how you hook readers. But make sure the rest of it lives up to the expectations that you've set.

- Write what you know. If you don't know something, learn it.

- Show, don't tell. If you show a character crying, the reader sees their tears, hears their sobs. If you tell them a character is crying, they won't experience it viscerally.

- Take time to look up anything you need to know, from minor grammar issues to big research questions. Make a note if it's going to take a lot of time and you need to come back to it.

- Don't forget to read as much as possible, and read widely.

- Carry a small notebook or get a writing app for your phone so you can jot down ideas when you're out and about.

- Eliminate distractions when you're writing, but try to learn to work in any environment.

- Pay attention to your process. Develop it.

- Stay healthy for optimum creativity and productivity. Eat well, exercise, and get plenty of sleep.

- Complete your projects. Push through the boring, tedious, and difficult phases of a project, and eventually, it will get fun and interesting again.

- Read everything you write aloud to check for flow. You'll also catch extra and missing words.

- Collect your writing tools and put together a kit that works for you. This isn't a literal tool kit—but you should know where everything is from your pens and notebooks to the things that inspire and motivate you.

- Include books on the craft in your writer's tool kit.

- Set some goals and then revisit them periodically to see if they need updating and to check your progress.

- Seek out your literary heroes. Follow writers you admire. Read and watch interviews. Find out what influenced them and how they succeeded.

- Make writing a priority.

- Be observant as you walk through the world. The smallest detail might be just the thing you need for a poem, story, or essay.

- Allow yourself to write poorly. The first draft is supposed to be rough, and sometimes you have to purge the bad writing before you can produce the good stuff.

- Pay attention to what inspires you. Bring more of that into your life.

- Watch out for verbiage, which is excess text that clutters up a piece of writing. Aim for clear, concise language.

- Mix and mingle with other writers. They'll motivate and inspire you, and you'll learn a lot from each other.

- Don't try too hard to be original.

- Redundancy means saying the same thing twice, unnecessarily, often in two different ways. Sometimes, repetition helps drive a point home, but redundancy is boring and distracting.

- Use your word processor's spelling and grammar checker, but don't rely on it. The system will sometimes get things wrong; it's not a replacement for a human editor.

- Don't overwhelm readers with unnecessary descriptions and details; however, make sure you include the most interesting and important details.

- You don't have to be a master of grammar, spelling, and punctuation, but you should make an effort to learn the basics and then expand on that knowledge over time.

- A writer is someone who writes. If you write, you're a writer.

Questions

Are there any tips you'd add to this list? Which of these tips do you think will serve you well in your writing? Have you already put any of them into practice?

55

Creative Writing Projects and Activities

One of the best things about creative writing is that there's never a shortage of activities to keep a writer engaged. I like to keep lists of writing projects, activities, prompts, and exercises. I refer to these lists when I'm feeling uninspired or unmotivated, when I'm between projects, and when I need a break from my regular writing routine. And sometimes, I just want to try something new.

Here are a bunch of my favorite writing (and writing-related) activities:

Poetry walk: Grab your notebook and put on your walking shoes. Take a stroll and make notes about what you see: city life or wildlife. Take photos to capture your surroundings. Pause during your walk (stop at a park bench or take a break at a coffee shop), and compose a poem or wait until you return home to do your writing.

Character diary: Fiction writers need to get inside their characters' heads. A great way to do this is to keep a diary as one of your characters. You'll learn to understand the character on a deeper level, and you'll find the character's voice.

Character Letters: A character diary gets you inside one character's head; letters help you infiltrate multiple characters' heads. Create an ongoing correspondence to explore character relationships and group dynamics within your cast. As an alternative, put your characters in a chat room.

Photo prompts: Head over to Google image search (or some other online image repository like Pinterest) to look for interesting photos that you can use to prompt a random creative writing session—this is a great way to find ideas for focused freewrites.

Take care of business: Take a break from your creative work and get down to business. Work on a query letter, a book proposal, or content for your author's website. Research the publishing industry, and plan your writing career.

What-if list: Some of the best writing ideas come from asking what-if questions. Make a big list of what-if questions that you can use later for writing inspiration.

Name game: You've got characters, story ideas, a novel in the works, and a blog. Conduct a brainstorming session to come up with names for characters, titles for books, and headlines for blog posts.

Make a chapbook: A chapbook is a little thematic collection of essays, stories, or poems (or all of these). Print copies and bring them to open mics and give readings, sell them through your local indie bookstore, or make an e-book and sell it or give it away online.

Daily writing spin: Set aside twenty minutes every day for one month to write in your journal or notebook. Write whatever you want during those twenty minutes; just make sure you do it every day. When the month is over, review what you've written. Do you see a theme? Can you harvest this material for some poems or a story?

Join a writer's group: You'll get feedback on your writing and make new friends. Other writers can offer support and share their knowledge and experience. Workshops are another excellent way to build your writing community.

Write for change: Find something you're passionate about and effect change through writing (a blog is great for this, but you can also submit to newspapers and magazines, or just send emails to friends and family).

Participate in NaNoWriMo: National Novel Writing Month happens every November, and you can spend the months before NaNo plotting, outlining, and sketching characters.

Study the craft: Select a book on the craft of writing, and read one chapter a day until you've finished it. Be sure to take notes. When you're done, make a list of things you've learned.

Make a collection: Pull together a collection of your finished works. Can you publish them in one volume? Submit them to magazines or agents? You could attend an open mic and read some of them to an audience. Keep your completed works in a convenient location in case opportunity strikes.

Start a blog: Give yourself a public space in which to write, put your voice out there, and stick to a regular writing schedule.

Personal statement: Why do you write? What do you love about writing? What are your goals? The very act of writing a personal statement will shed light on an otherwise murky path.

Reimagine your favorite story: Take an old legend or fairy tale, and give it a modern twist. Start with an outline, and if your concept works, develop it into a short story, novel, or screenplay, or write a poem or essay about it.

Submit something: If you've produced a lot of writing over the years, there's a good chance you have a few publishable pieces. Why keep them hidden away?

Get personal: Write a polished personal essay about an experience you've had that you think is worth sharing. If the project intrigues you, let it expand into a memoir, or fictionalize it and turn it into a novel.

Try something new: If you always write fiction, try to write a song lyric. If you're focused on poetry, try writing a personal essay. Change genres: if you're a romance writer, give science fiction a spin.

Read everything you've ever written: Go through all your files and notebooks. You'll see that your writing has improved over time, and you may find some old projects that are worth dusting off and revisiting.

Find seven writing exercises that intrigue you. and then set aside twenty minutes a day for a week to tackle those writing exercises. When you're done, make a list of things you learned. Can you turn any of those exercises into a bigger project, like a short story or a poem? A book?

Watch a writerly movie: There are tons of great films about writers. Here are a few to get you started: *Misery, Stranger Than Fiction,* and *Throw Mama from the Train.*

Read: Grab a memoir, pick up a novel, or read a screenplay. Try a genre you've never read before.

Make a five-year plan for your writing: Work out your writing goals for the next five years.

Word puzzles: Word puzzles are a fun way to build your vocabulary!

Support writers: Spend some time supporting fellow writers. Promote them on social media, or post a review on Amazon or Goodreads. Head down to your favorite indie bookstore, and buy their books.

Attend a literary event: Look for poetry readings, book signings, or lectures in your area. These events are a lot more fun and interesting than they sound.

Memory Prompts: Grab an old photo album or flip through the photos on your phone—or use recall to bring up memories that you can write about. Use this as an exercise in writing description or crafting a narrative about something you experienced or witnessed.

Book club: Join a book club. You'll get exposure to new and interesting works that you otherwise might not have read, and you'll meet people who are passionate about literature.

Learn a new skill: There are lots of skills you can master to give your writing practice or career a boost: blog technology, social media strategies, query letter guidelines, copyright laws, marketing, and interview techniques.

Read aloud: Let's say you get published. You might have to do a book tour; you'll probably do local signings. Even if you self-publish and do all your marketing online, you might have to do phone or video interviews. You might even want to record your own audiobook. So practice.

Observation Station: Grab your notebook or journal and head to a heavily populated area. Park yourself on a bench or in a comfy café and do a little people watching. Record your observations and brainstorm ways you can use observation to influence and empower your writing.

Questions

What are some of your favorite creative writing activities? Which of these projects listed in this chapter would you be willing to try?

56

Go Forth and Write

The writing life is unlike any other. Writers spend a lot of time alone, with only our words and ideas to keep us company. We're idea seekers—always looking for the next topic, poem, or plot. Every moment is an experience that could lead to a masterpiece, so every moment is a masterpiece. We live as observers, taking in the world around us so we can immortalize the best parts of it in our writing. We're communicators, using words to forge connections. It's not enough to tell a story or share an experience. We want to show readers what it was like to be there, to live it, even if it never really happened.

Our work is play, and our play is work. We breathe language. We engage in make-believe. We search for stories that beg to be told. We contemplate words and images, grammar and structure, the historical and the fantastical, fact and fiction (and the difference between the two). We get excited over things that put other people to sleep—a passionate voice, a riveting scene, a complex character. We are delighted by stationery and writing instruments, tools that other people see as mundane necessities. And while we may be concerned with ordinary living, we live an extraordinary life.

All these things make up the life of a writer, the writing lifestyle.

Creative writing is an adventure, and it's an adventure that is threaded throughout every minute of a writer's day. I hope you will find all the tools and techniques to make this adventure rewarding and meaningful. If you make a commitment to writing, you will be able to weather the dry spells and ride out the challenges—from grammar conundrums to writer's block and everything in between.

The work we do matters, even if we never show it to another living soul. The sheer act of creation is therapeutic, and the feeling of having written—of having created something that is uniquely ours—is meaningful.

May your writing adventure be fulfilling! And may you keep writing, always.

Afterword

Thank you for reading *Ready, Set, Write: A Guide to Creative Writing* from the Adventures in Writing series. The next book in the series is *101 Creative Writing Exercises*, which provides exercises that stimulate creativity while imparting useful techniques for writing fiction, poetry, and creative nonfiction. You can also pick up *1200 Creative Writing Prompts*, which is packed with poetry prompts, story starters, and ideas for nonfiction writing projects.

If you'd like to be notified when new books on the craft of writing are published, sign up for my newsletter at writingforward.com/subscribe. As a subscriber, you'll get exclusive offers, creative writing tips, and other goodies.

If you enjoyed this book, please consider leaving a review online. Help other writers by telling them why you found this book beneficial. Reviews also help authors sell more books, and that frees us up to write more of them.

Finally, please visit my website at writingforward.com. It's packed with creative writing tips and ideas, plus exercises and prompts to keep your pen moving. You can also follow Writing Forward on social media:

Twitter: twitter.com/writingforward.

Facebook: facebook.com/writingforward.

Pinterest: pinterest.com/writingforward.

Thanks again for reading this book. I hope your adventure in writing is fulfilling. Keep writing!

References

Books

Angelou, Maya. *I Know Why the Caged Bird Sings*. New York: Random House, 1969.

Collins, Suzanne. The Hunger Games Trilogy. New York: Scholastic Press, 2008–2010.

Crichton, Michael. *Jurassic Park.* New York: Knopf, 1990.

Rowling, J. K. Harry Potter Series. New York: Scholastic, 1998–2007.

Steinbeck, John. *The Grapes of Wrath*. Reissue ed. New York: Penguin Group, 2006.

Poetry

Angelou, Maya. "Caged Bird." *The Complete Collected Poems of Maya Angelou*. New York: Random House, 1994.

Dunbar, Paul Laurence. "Sympathy." *The Collected Poetry of Paul Laurence Dunbar*. Edited by Joanne M. Braxton. Charlottesville: University of Virginia Press, 1993.

Marlowe, Christopher. "The Passionate Shepherd to His Love." Poetry Foundation. Accessed February 19, 2019. https://www.poetryfoundation.org/poems/44675/the-passionate-shepherd-to-his-love.

Raleigh, Sir Walter. "The Nymph's Reply to the Shepherd." Poetry Foundation. Accessed February 19, 2019. https://www.poetryfoundation.org/poems/44939/the-nymphs-reply-to-the-shepherd.

Williams, William Carlos. "The Red Wheelbarrow." Poetry Foundation. Accessed February 19, 2019.

https://www.poetryfoundation.org/poems/45502/the-red-wheelbarrow.

Film

Alice in Wonderland (3-D). Directed by Tim Burton. Los Angeles: Walt Disney Studios Motion Pictures, 2010.

Alice in Wonderland. Produced by Walt Disney. Los Angeles: RKO Radio Pictures, 1951.

Star Wars: The Force Awakens. Directed by J.J. Abrams. Los Angeles: Walt Disney Studios Motion Pictures, 2015.

Star Wars: The Original Trilogy. Directed by George Lucas. Los Angeles: 20th Century Fox, 1977-1983.

Interviews

Margolis, Rick. "A Killer Story: An Interview with Suzanne Collins, Author of 'The Hunger Games.'" *School Library Journal.* Accessed February 19, 2019. https://www.slj.com/?detailStory=a-killer-story-an-interview-with-suzanne-collins-author-of-the-hunger-games.

About the Author

Melissa Donovan is the founder and editor of Writing Forward, a blog packed with creative writing tips and ideas. She is the author of the Adventures in Writing series and the Storyteller's Toolbox series, as well as various works of fiction and poetry.

Melissa started writing poetry and song lyrics at age thirteen. Shortly thereafter, she began keeping a journal. She studied at Sonoma State University, earning a BA in English with a concentration in creative writing. Since then, Melissa has worked as an author, copywriter, professional blogger, and writing coach.

Writing Forward

Writing Forward features creative writing tips, ideas, tools, and techniques, as well as writing exercises and prompts that offer inspiration and help build skills.

To get more writing tips and ideas and to receive notifications when new books on the craft of writing are released, visit Writing Forward: www.writingforward.com.

Made in the USA
Las Vegas, NV
17 August 2021